VALUED
DAUGHTERS

VALUED DAUGHTERS

FIRST-GENERATION CAREER WOMEN

ALICE W. CLARK

⑤SAGE www.sagepublishing.com

Los Angeles | London | New Delhi | Singapore | Washington DC | Melbourne

First published in 2016 by

SAGE Publications India Pvt Ltd
B1/I-1 Mohan Cooperative Industrial Area
Mathura Road, New Delhi 110 044, India
www.sagepub.in

SAGE Publications Inc
2455 Teller Road
Thousand Oaks, California 91320, USA

SAGE Publications Ltd
1 Oliver's Yard, 55 City Road
London EC1Y 1SP, United Kingdom

SAGE Publications Asia-Pacific Pte Ltd
3 Church Street
#10-04 Samsung Hub
Singapore 049483

Published by Vivek Mehra for SAGE Publications India Pvt Ltd, typeset in 11/13 pts Garamond by PrePSol Enterprises Pvt Ltd and printed at Chaman Enterprises, New Delhi.

Library of Congress Cataloging-in-Publication Data

Names: Clark, Alice Whitcomb, author.
Title: Valued daughters : first-generation career women / Alice W. Clark.
Description: New Delhi, India ; Thousand Oaks, California : SAGE, 2016. |
   Includes bibliographical references and index.
Identifiers: LCCN 2015049011 | ISBN 9789351508885 (hardback : alk. paper) |
   ISBN 9789351508878 (epub) | ISBN 9789351508861 (ebook)
Subjects: LCSH: Women in the professions–India. | Women employees–India. |
   Women college graduates–Employment–India. | Young
   women–Employment–India. | Career development–India.
Classification: LCC HD6054.2.I4 C53 2016 | DDC 331.40954–dc23 LC record
available at http://lccn.loc.gov/2015049011

ISBN: 978-93-515-0888-5 (HB)

The SAGE Team: Aditi Chopra, Sandhya Gola and Vinitha Nair

Dedicated to the women of India,
past, present, and future

Thank you for choosing a SAGE product!
If you have any comment, observation or feedback,
I would like to personally hear from you.
Please write to me at **contactceo@sagepub.in**

Vivek Mehra, Managing Director and CEO,
SAGE Publications India Pvt Ltd, New Delhi

Bulk Sales

SAGE India offers special discounts
for purchase of books in bulk.
We also make available special imprints
and excerpts from our books on demand.

For orders and enquiries, write to us at

Marketing Department
SAGE Publications India Pvt Ltd
B1/I-1, Mohan Cooperative Industrial Area
Mathura Road, Post Bag 7
New Delhi 110044, India

E-mail us at **marketing@sagepub.in**

Get to know more about SAGE

Be invited to SAGE events, get on our mailing list.
Write today to **marketing@sagepub.in**

This book is also available as an e-book.

Contents

List of Tables

Acknowledgments

This work could have never been imagined or carried out if it had not been for the long-standing friendship, intellectual engagement, and material support of Veena Poonacha and Vibhuti Patel in Mumbai; T. V. Sekher in Bengaluru and Mumbai; Tulsi Patel in Delhi; Sumita Parmar in Allahabad; and Pamela Price in many locations up to the present, starting in Madison during our graduate school years.

There are others to whom I am also grateful for their assistance: in Allahabad, Ruchika Varma and Satendra Kumar; in Mumbai, Kamala Ganesh, Madhushree Sekher, and Amrita Gupta; in Vadodara, Amita Pandya, Lancy Lobo, and Harendra Choksi; in Delhi, Shelly Tara, Manjeet Bhatia, Rajni Palriwala, Preet Rustagi, Pamela Philipose, and Sonalde Desai; and in Berkeley, Raka Ray, Cynthia Lloyd, and Lawrence Cohen. I thank Anil Inamdar of the American Institute of Indian Studies for his energetic assistance with research affiliation formalities. I thank the Indian Institute for Advanced Study and the Women's Studies and Development Centre at the University of Delhi, for inviting me to present part of this work at a seminar on "Locating Gender in the New Middle Class" in Shimla in March 2014, and the Research Centre for Women's Studies at SNDT Women's University, for the invitation to speak at "Feminist Historiography" seminar in Mumbai in February 2015. For thoughtful guidance, I appreciate the editorial team at the Delhi office of SAGE Publications. And, I salute the University of California Library for being the finest research library of my acquaintance in any part of the world.

I thank my family—Charles and our two daughters, their husbands, and our first grandson—for their companionship, care, and lively interest over the years, including traveling to India for the 2013–2014 Christmas holidays to provide me a breather in the midst of my research stay. I look affectionately back into the past at the two generations of India-involved family before our own, and forward into the future at two emerging new ones.

1

Intersecting Transitions

The book sets out to trace a finite moment in a sweeping transition, the spread of ambitions among young graduate women for lifetime careers in urban India. The larger process is made up of several intersecting transitions—demographic, educational, economic, and social—each of which has its own history and trajectory. Yet there is another transition embedded within these—an emerging and changing sense of self among young women, one that is flexible, capacious, agreeable, and cooperative, yet firmly focused on freedom. The finite moment, occurring in various forms and in scattered urban locations across India in the early 21st century, is illustrated in multitude of stories, reflecting both a delicate balancing act and a surge of determination. These are stories motivated by well-laid plans, held by young women and their parents, to make a partial but powerful change in the gender expectations of the past. The transition is thus a historical one, bringing together the life plans of two or three generations of people, with roots reaching even further back into the past.

My project has been to understand the aspirations of a small subset of the current generation of college-going women, and to learn how and why their aspirations differ from those of earlier generations of their peers. These daughters appear to be valued by their natal families for a wider variety of reasons than similarly placed daughters previously were. This project, then, contributes to a developing literature on where, and to what extent, gendered social change may be currently happening in India.

The book is based on research carried out in late 2013 and early 2014, when I collected interview data in three Indian cities from young women aged 17–25 who were studying in college or postgraduate programs and planning on lifetime careers, and whose mothers had never had one. This last qualification was an important filter, maintained across all those selected for interviews, for the purpose of understanding intergenerational changes in urban female aspirations. Each research subject was introduced to me by one of her professors. The university sites chosen for the research were in Allahabad, Mumbai, and Vadodara. Interviews collected in these cities are then placed in relation to others which were collected from some students and some young employees in an earlier research project in Bengaluru (previously Bangalore; Clark and Sekher 2007).

The total size of my sample is only an average of eight in each city, an infinitesimal amount, seemingly providing absolutely unrepresentative anecdotes. These are not full ethnographies; they can comprise only a sketch. Yet this examination of a small, focused, and nonrandom sample is meant to provide a useful approach to consider important issues in the study of social change. The idea of transitions that intersect with one another is somewhat different from the points of view taken by many other studies of Indian social phenomena, one which can be seen as an experiment in social history and social historical demography. This is meant to be a research effort in what I would call *qualitative social demography*. Supported by some secondary data analysis, it constitutes an exploration to see if qualitative and quantitative research methods can be better combined when trying to understand women's history and unfolding present circumstances. Such an experiment may prove to be important to consider because demographic research is so quantitative, while women's studies research tends to be intensely qualitative.

An approach that is both nuanced and yet broad is needed to gain perspective on the changing motivations of young women, the role of college education in impacting their career goals and their marital and reproductive plans, and the elements that make up female autonomy and agency. Beyond what this book can attempt to fulfill, but can only suggest, is the need for ethnographies of educated women's social and economic behaviors, with their various and conflicting motivations, at highly disaggregated levels like neighborhoods, castes, villages, tribes, and religious groups. Different groups of women who are currently getting educated may have different levels of choice about their careers, marriages, and future. How are their choices shaped or constrained by the web of relationships in which they are embedded? How are changes in their choices being shaped by historical forces that are still unfolding? What effects do their choices have on the overall system of social reproduction, which may provide us with a more comprehensive picture of demographic and social change as it is occurring?

I approach these questions by interviewing young women in college, looking forward to having lifelong careers. In the effort to understand a generational shift in gender relations that is going on in some families regarding young women's professional aspirations, seen in light of the varied social locations these families inhabit, two basic focus areas have emerged. Understanding this generational shift seems to call for (a) a focus on new kinds of subject and identity formation taking place among young women as part of their college education process, and (b) an analysis of what kinds of families are now sponsoring their daughters' lifetime career ambitions, and why. An earlier notion that this generational shift as young women's career aspirations would be mainly an upper middle class phenomenon is not borne out by the research. Class enters into the framework along a wide spectrum, ranging from some class locations of relative privilege to others of urgent need. The research has also undermined an initial notion that upper-caste status would be nearly universal among career-oriented young women.

The one-hour interviews I had with female students took place one-on-one, often in a college classroom we had to ourselves. I pursued a list of questions with them about their education, career plans, parents' circumstances, family support, future marriage plans, desires for children, planned usage of money they earned, thoughts on work–family balance, and ideas about the nature of professionalism. For some interviewees, when it became possible, a home visit followed with the daughter present to help translate and/or add to her parents' comments. I was not bound by my questionnaire and did not force a return to it if the conversation moved to other areas subjects wanted to share. In every case, the research subject was eager to participate. Research subjects and their families were informed that their names would be changed, and that some details would be omitted or altered to protect them from identification. The interview material was arranged into blocks of text that did not reflect the uneven way the conversations actually developed, but that stay true to the life narratives, which were shared.

Theoretically, a combination of the ideas of Sen and Bourdieu is of particular interest for this project. Both thinkers deal with the effects, benefits, and drawbacks of education, so that their works are appropriately applicable to a project where higher education plays a central role. Amartya Sen (1999, 2009; also see Agarwal 2005) is famously noted for stressing both personal and the overall social and economic effects of enhancing people's freedom and developing their capabilities and choices. Education is one of the most potentially enhancing factors in this theory. Pierre Bourdieu (1977, 2010; and with Passeron [2000]), by contrast, is known for his analysis of social props and barriers under the label of cultural capital, governed within the individual by a set of predilections that he labels as the habitus. These nearly unconscious usages lurk beneath the surface, either hobbling or helping in enabling the fulfillment of ambitions and social aspirations that people associate with becoming educated.

In Sen's *Development as Freedom* (1999), there is a chapter, "Women's Agency and Social Change," in which he sees women as "dynamic promoters of social transformations that can alter the lives of both women and men." Touching on key issues we are exploring in this study, he writes,

> [t]he relative respect and regard for women's well-being is strongly in-fluenced by such variables as women's ability to earn an independent income, to find employment outside the home, to have ownership rights and to have literacy and be educated participants in decisions within and outside the family.

Two important outcomes can result from having literate and educated women earning their own incomes, he believes—this can enhance "the social standing of a woman in the household and the society," and "women's agency and voice, influenced by education and employment, can in turn influence the nature of the public discussion." More than 15 years after this influential work of Sen's, in the present study we are in a position to form an impression of recent social transformations that have been motivated by young urban women gaining education in the hope of obtaining educated, professional level employment. We are able to ask in detail how these transformations have recently affected women's standing within their households, and then to consider briefly how they may be influencing the public discussion on many issues.

In *Distinction* (2010), Bourdieu draws a picture of the refinements that people lack if not brought up with them, such as a fine taste in classical music. This type of knowledge and formed taste are seen as distinguishing persons seeking positions, whether in employment or in society and politics, from one another, to the point where the more refined candidates may win these contests. These cultural distinctions may read as slightly archaic in relation to today's societies. A taste for classical Indian music was richly cultivated in past decades in elite Indian families (Chaudhuri 2009), and their offspring's social and employment advantages may have been partly connected with this refinement. But the sense of high culture versus low culture drawn by Bourdieu has faded in this current markedly neoliberal era, with its instant online global interconnections, fashions, and fads. Added to a picture of Bourdieu as the author of a complex theory of cultural capital in the construction and reproduction of class, I would also draw attention to a more colloquial notion that has burst these boundaries, lost or forgotten its roots in Bourdieu, and is used more widely. In writings connected with race and caste relations, particularly, without any citation, notions of cultural and social capital are widely and rather loosely used to reference traits and abilities inbred from childhood, based on advantages held and imparted by people's natal families. Either in a close reading of Bourdieu or in a more colloquial use, the concept of cultural capital and its formation are very important and, in a wide variety of current literatures, quite inevitable.

In looking at the stories collected, I have also been reminded of "modernization theory," a loose construct that has been used for many decades with the contents of the "modern" shifting across time frames. It is a framework of which I am quite critical, as will be detailed throughout the book. One of its abiding interests has been a notion called female autonomy, which is hard to pin down (as lucidly discussed by Basu 1996), but which has been seen as an instrumentalist variable, leading mainly to the accomplishment of goals outside itself. In its very instrumentality, it fits oddly but aptly into several other theoretical possibilities. To give an important example, one may fruitfully use postcolonial feminist theoretical constructs in disclosing the new forms of oppression and patriarchal hegemony that clearly still circumscribe the freedoms of the young subjects whose stories I am collecting. In the bulk of this book, however, I am interested in elucidating the liberatory potential of these stories, which appears richly to exist in some, though truncated in others. The limitations of the stories and the hopes they express, as well as their portents for the future, will be discussed as the narratives proceed.

Ideas elaborated in Sen and Nussbaum's capabilities approach (Nussbaum 2001, 2011; Nussbaum and Sen 1993; Sen 1999, 2009) give rise to a term I have found it useful to coin in this work. Using their framework as a springboard, I identify an assertiveness capability, vividly demonstrated by the young women still in college whom I interviewed, and I view it as a realized source of moral force and personal identity creation in itself. I discuss the limitations that such a capability may contain. With reference to Bourdieu (1977, 2010), I address forms of social and cultural capital as they bear on a discussion of how gender relations can be changed or entrenched, and evaluate which of these tendencies I believe is the stronger. Toward the end of the book, I undertake to spell out my understanding of ways in which a long-standing system of social reproduction is now undergoing alteration, and to add my judgment of ways that this process is larger than may have been envisioned in other feminist work.

The narrative perspective is one closely focused on female career aspirations, parental support, and the future family formation strategies that young women believe would support them in maintaining a career. The aspirations that are now being fulfilled are those of the parents for their daughters to be educated and prepared for careers. The further aspirations, whose fulfillment is as yet unpredictable, are those of the young women themselves to actualize and fulfill their goals of having careers for a lifetime. These two sets of aspirations, by the parents and by their daughters, are somewhat different, but they add together to create a structure that supports the valuing of the daughter as an agent. We will examine how in each case she also remains an embedded agent.

This is a book about young women who (so far) have been uniquely lucky. Their stories contrast most cruelly with those of girls, so much less privileged in residential location and family sensibility, who do not get to continue in school even to the secondary level, when they long to do so (Majumdar 2011: 212–236). The good luck of my research subjects is made up not only of their urban residence, with its broad exposure to multiple possibilities, and their families' support for them, based on particular family needs and hopes; these young women have also been very successful students, fortunate in the favor in which they are held by their professors and mentors. Additionally, they have all studied in English medium colleges, and that is the language in which this research was conducted.

The discrimination in my study against all the other kinds of female students who exist adds up to a kind of elitism of focus. I put this on the table forthrightly, so that critics may ask why these fortunate and rather exceptional girls are important to look at in considering societal change. My answer is that, even with all their luck so far, they represent, by way of the filter of mothers who never worked, a certain slice of ordinary urban middle class families or would-be middle class families as predominantly found in these same cities just a generation ago. Mothers who did not work were the standard in the vast majority of urban middle class families in previous years. The families of my subjects in the late 20th century were not ones in which the preponderance of members were either very highly educated or cosmopolitan. Some of the families I examine were elite in caste, class, or both, though others were not, but none had figured in the ranks of female professionalism in the past.

This book ultimately attempts to locate and to project forward some elements of a path toward greater gender equity for young women living in cities, loyal to their families of origin, hopeful of finding an appropriate fit within their families-to-be, and yet trying to become professionals. I foresee many daunting challenges that the young women I have met face: finding jobs they like; marrying either by choice or by arrangement into families that are supportive (or even defying the requirement to marry); building a loving and helpful partnership; controlling their own income cooperatively with their partners; managing career and family successfully; negotiating with the players at home; dealing skillfully with the workplace and with the development of their careers; and navigating all the spaces between home and work safely. None of these challenges are researched in this book; they are simply recognized as imminent. What is researched in this book is how a young woman who is getting an education and planning for a career today, usually with the full support of her parents, is constructing her own self-identity; and with that process of self-awareness and self-reflection begun, how she hopes to make a contribution to the world that is different, that is new, and that is her own.

There is much to say about the relentless female education transition that is taking place in India, just as it is across the globe. This will be undertaken in detail in Chapter 3. But first, I acknowledge that statements about transitions often appear to bring us perilously close to the teleological temptation inherent in what is known as modernization theory. This theory seems to posit an endpoint to processes and transitions, which it spotlights, as though the world were hurtling toward a situation of modernity, which attains a certain high point much to be longed for. Certainly, we may long for, and strongly advocate, the education and empowerment of women, the eradication of poverty, the spread of justice for every community, the ending of violence against women, the development of employment opportunities, and a much more adequate environment and societal infrastructure for the nurture of children and for human flourishing than is found in India today.[1] But not all apparently progressive social and economic tendencies are commensurate with the objectives just stated. Some, in fact, are harmful and threatening in the first degree. In a teleological modernization framework, however, there can be an unjustified temptation to project some kind of near-perfection's eventual arrival.

---

[1] Such issues are also found in a great many countries of the world today. The list of countries to which this longing pertains would be lengthy, but they are not the subject of the present book.

I disclaim a romanticized expectation regarding the future for women and societies, by stating my standpoint as a historian, watching the unfolding of the present in light of the recent past, the remembered past, and the recorded past, rather than with any sense of presaging a particular future. I dislodge the teleological temptation by stating that my view of the future, as contrasted with modernization theory, is one that holds great hope and serious pessimism in balance. Ideologically and analytically, I hold a feminist position, giving priority to the study of historically based changes that benefit women and girls, and that may benefit those yet to be born. But these changes will not be the solution to all of society's problems, not even those most closely concerning women. I disavow the kind of vision that imagines that they will.

The feminist approaches I claim should be outlined here further. I begin with the analytical approaches I attach to my use of the word feminism, and move later to the ideology.

Feminist historiography and feminist social history as analytical lenses are somewhat rarely mingled with social demography. Social demography, in turn, is an analytical lens that is not often focused on feminist social anthropology or history in studies of gender in Indian society. An important exception has been a very productive line of examinations of differential sex ratios across India (Das Gupta 2009; Das Gupta and Bhat 1997; Das Gupta and Shuzhou 1999; Guilmoto 2009; Jeffery 2014; Kaur 2008; Miller 1981; Patel 2007; and Sekher and Hatti 2010, among many others). However, I am training these same lenses together in a different way, attempting to blend them in a study of individual female lives that are being lived, as opposed to being lost. I suggest that to do so is an important and much-needed approach.

Any current feminist analytical orientation involves a well-developed set of complex and overlapping views. One of the most fruitful of these as a background to this study, which attempts to conduct both secondary data analysis and primary qualitative narrative examination, is intersectionality. This perspective claims that we cannot understand either the obstacles people confront, or the advantages they enjoy, by classifying them in groups within a few of the structures that impinge upon their lives. Structures of social class, economic level, race, religion, sexuality, nationality, ethnicity, and caste intersect in multiple ways with each other, and then with gender in an even more complex set of ways, as is widely recognized in feminist studies today. Feminist studies which analyze gender systems are now retitled by many practitioners as Women's and Gender Studies, or simply Gender Studies. Such a title encourages the analysis of masculinities as well as femininities, including nonconforming gender identities and expressions, and most importantly, allows us to deconstruct the gender binary. These huge advances in the analysis of gender, based on the understanding of it as a malleable social construct, are recognized in labeling my approach as feminist. In this study, exploring the workings of a gender system in a certain social arena, I privilege those unique categories that are found among my subjects. This leaves to others a more comprehensive coverage of gender and its intersectionality in a wider set of segments of society.

An ideological claim to feminism is simpler to state than analytical perspectives. "Feminism is the radical notion that women are people." Though not knowing where this motto originated, I adopt it wholeheartedly. In opposition to the powerful social construct that we call gender, women are equal human beings, who must come to be dealt with as no less than fully equal to men. This is a human rights perspective, given formal expression in the Universal Declaration of Human Rights, a towering document of the 20th century which the 21st has very far to go in fully adopting and implementing. In some ways, and in some social and political locations, the very distance between that declaration and its fulfillment seems to widen in the conditions of our current world.

In embracing a human rights lens on feminism, the perspective of this study is greatly enriched by Sen's work. Sen's view of humans as flourishing best within the freedom to select the "things they have reason to value" is a view that gives a green light to human rights. Rights both to education and to the ability to obtain valuable work are included in several articles in the Universal Declaration of Human Rights as basic human rights. Neither of these rights implies, nor is either of them defined in the declaration as being equal to, complete personal autonomy. When people are provided with particularly supportive relationships and circumstances, however, these very rights can come to be seen as being congruent with an embedded autonomy. Much of what people have reasons to value, in fact, derives from their embedded situation within their relationships. The basic question then becomes: Do these relationships, or do they not, support and enhance women's freedoms to choose the things that are of value to them?

The feminist approach of this book also owes much to Bourdieu, observing the very real limits that people's situations place on the wider circles they are trying to open up around themselves. Both these situational limits and acts of resistance to them are important to think about in our examination of gender roles. Patterns within a given woman's culturally constructed habitus may either consciously or subconsciously dictate how she ought to behave, at the same time that she is acting to shape creative variations on those very same themes. People are sometimes more fully conscious than Bourdieu seems to allow, though I find the habitus to be a powerfully suggestive concept, one which is quite inescapable, in fact. The process of creation of new cultural capital, however, shown in some of the stories told in this book, while clearly due in large part to external changes in underlying social and economic structures, is also a very artful one. Individually it requires cleverness and even craftiness on a young woman's part so as to follow accepted forms, even while maneuvering within them, so that the self can feel more fully free.

Closely held between the invisible constraining social limits within a person, a la Bourdieu, and a sense of empowering freedom, a la Sen (which, under the considerations I have just given, both may characterize a person who is seeking things she has reason to value), there is a space. In this space there can emerge an adventure in self-identity creation. One can only strive to become, however, what one first imagines being. There are limits to this, in the sense that models are essential to people's ambitions: people can much better imagine becoming like someone they know or have heard about, than becoming something alien to either their experience or their frame of reference. Most people cannot imagine becoming something unheard of, that is; following some of the patterns set by others is very helpful. Young people may "idolize" certain others, setting them up as models;

their idols sometimes even reach out and beckon them towards the patterns they are setting. In this book, we discuss an intergenerational genealogy of female influence. We witness, as well, the optimistic hopes of current-day fathers and mothers as they watch their daughters' capabilities unfold, and take account, too, of the warmly encouraging sponsorship and guidance of their mentors and professors. These are novel sets of patterns, to which some young women are now able to attach themselves, contesting customary patterns of female habitus. It is within this context that we will discuss what I am calling the current-day professional imaginary.

My interpretation of the interviews owes a debt to years spent teaching modern world history, and to pastimes reading and rereading classic novels of the late nineteenth and early 20th century. Female characters in those books seek chances to comprehend their circumstances; rarely are they without at least partial insight into the overwhelming contexts constraining them. They follow certain lodestars, using help they may find along the way, and their resistance to the limits is often registered in a very inward way, in statements they make to themselves, as well as to others if they do share them with others. The most strategic of these characters pursue a kind of conversation with themselves that I would call, simply, "thinking things through." Novels published before the First World War illuminated an earlier world order and its gender outcomes (see Hobsbawn's history trilogy, 1962, 1975, 1987, which never omits gender effects of historical change): it was a socio-political global order that I see as being highly relevant to the lives of women in recent decades in many regions, as well as in India.

In recent literature, the hard anvil between circumstances and thought in Indian women's lives has been brilliantly hammered out in the stories of Mahasweta Devi (Bardhan 1990). The clash between deeper democratization and outrageous injustice in our current period is calling upon more people from more backgrounds than ever before to think things through, both inwardly and outwardly. Thinking things through has never been more relevant than it is today.

The rest of this introduction provides a short description of what each chapter sets out to do. In Chapter 2, we look at the ways in which female career ambition has had a long genealogy, reaching far back into the past. We hear a few rather haunting stories of educated women of several successive generations, who had their hopes and struggles and some successes in the past. And we examine, using a variety of data, why female career ambition has reaped such extremely small rewards up to very recent years, in spite of the ever-increasing stress on female education.

Chapter 3 looks at the way demographic changes have played a major role in shaping gender relations in the past and are doing so now. There are personal stories that especially illuminate the large and painful role of mortality in warping the structure of families and fully challenging the ingenuity of women. We then look at historical changes impacting the long-standing paradox represented by sex ratios. The theme of women's rapidly increasing share of higher education is illustrated and then problematized.

In Chapter 4, we examine four unique cities and their educational cultures in relation to the experiences of the young women studying in them: Allahabad, Mumbai, Vadodara, and Bengaluru. The ambiance of the city rubs off on each student, filtered through the atmosphere of very particular universities, with their long traditions and ideals. The students I have met experience both hopes and sometimes also confusions about their futures as they absorb these influences. Their families, whether present or far away, sometimes also seem to be having mixed experiences of new hope and new confusion. In this chapter, we examine this dynamic.

In Chapter 5, some discoveries that this research has made through the interviewing process are explored. There are categories that were not used as prerequisites to the interview sample that nevertheless proved to be very important in most of the cases. First, it is apparent that fathers play a key role in positively influencing the career hopes and expectations that their daughters hold. In some cases, a daughter is being urgently solicited by both parents to study for and plan on a career, due to needs her family hopes she can meet for them and based on her having already compiled a promising academic record. In almost all cases, the father's support is predominant. Secondly, we examine particularly the salient role of birth order, along with other key aspects of completed family composition, in influencing the career expectations these families have come to have for their daughters.

In Chapter 6, we attempt to analyze the conundrum of the increasing numbers of young educated urban women who are reaching for careers, in light of the lagging performance of the labor market. We examine the privileged part that women belonging to long-standing elites continue to play in a changing opportunity structure for women. And in contrast to each young woman's hopes, we assess the issues around the gender roles that are and will continue to be still expected of them, even as female professionalism takes hold more widely.

In Chapter 7, we ask about the gains and losses and even the drawbacks attending women's newly envisioned horizons for their ambitions. We look at the uninterrupted embeddedness of female agency in commitments to family, which is to be found in a sample constructed in the way this one is. The varying ways that other scholars have been researching this family embeddedness are examined, putting this book in a comparative context.

In Chapter 8, we look once again at the women whose stories have been considered, this time more particularly in light of the way in which they have become caught up in a new professional imaginary. This vision is found to characterize women located in both old and new middle classes, and so we examine some ideas on the development of these classes. The chapter then puts forth a theory of social reproduction as it begins to undergo systemic change. Finally, it undertakes to draw a picture of the emerging form of self-identity that is being shaped and molded by young urban women, and to project the implications of this development for their future and for the future of families and society.

Chapter 9 looks back once again at history and forward toward the future, in considering a kind of march toward gender justice that threads through time. We cannot be assured that such a desired state of being will come into existence, but this final chapter draws up a vision of a path that might lead to it.

2

A History of Women among Men

What self-identities have been claimed by Indian educated women over time? I seek here to locate within a rough time frame the kinds of identities educated women have wanted to claim for themselves, above and beyond those that areas assigned to them according to their group, family, religious, and caste or ethnic affiliations. To do so is, of course, a fraught project: people claim identities and develop subjectivity and a sense of selfhood within a social context, and this holds true no less for men than women. Too, in India the very concept of the self is a grand one, swathed in universal principles. From the smallest and most quotidian detail of who one is and what one does, to the largest cognitive possibility in the universe, the concept of the self is richly scripted. Yet, even so, to approach subjectivity and longed-for self-identities from the perspective of the subject is my aim.

The kinds of new female identities to be focused on, from the vantage point of the interviews reported on in the following chapters, relate most specifically to the contemporary longing of young educated women to become professionals. Increasing numbers of families are encouraging daughters not only to become college educated but also, if they wish and are qualified to do so, to enter lifelong careers. What is the role of the family, and what is the agency of the daughter? How does an emerging young adult identify herself in this context? What kind of identity, or blend of identities, can she hope for? What part of this process embodies genuine aspirations of her own? We examine these questions throughout this book with a view to better understanding the subjectivities of young college-educated urban women, especially those expressions of their subjectivity that have become externalized and made socially visible in the form of new career orientations.

What is the history of this ambition for a career, and how do women's longings interface with social positions that women have occupied in a patriarchal social structure? Chatterjee (1989) tied up in a rather convincing package the painful contradiction of women's attempted advances during the nation's freedom struggle, being then constrained within a powerful structure of disabling limitations powered by a male-dominated nationalism. And Sinha (in Sarkar and Sarkar 2007) has built upon this to show us discrete cases of establishing a putative "voice" in the supposed person of "the" Indian woman, tied up in one or another symbol. However, we need not leave our study of women's historically changing identities caught up only in these structural and ideological trammels, I would argue. We can also glimpse an emerging multi-generational process of influence and suggestion regarding alternative identities that women could consider, starting with the period during and after the struggle for India's freedom. In those eras, new kinds of lives became possible for some women, however few, in terms of professional workforce participation. The fact that they were, indeed, very few, will be reiterated and even enumerated in detail below. And yet, their lives had a ripple effect. I consider here the flow of influences this statement implies.

It is worth looking at the newness found in some early and mid-20th-century women's lives, in judging the long-range effects they have continued to have on women's aspirations. This moves us through several generations and into the most recent ones. We start with the freedom struggle generation, move through the daughters of Independence generation (as in Liddle and Joshi 1986), and then locate women who were young in the 1980s and 1990s. In future chapters, we consider in detail the thoughts of some young women living in four particular Indian cities today.[1] To ultimately focus closely

---

[1] Allahabad, Mumbai, Vadodara, and Bengaluru.

on current-day women's aspirations, this chapter first explores what we can glean about the past history of educated women's aspirations for self-identity. The nature of what educated women have been seeking in this regard has changed over time.

A number of elite families—that is, upper-caste or upper-class families, in which some of the men were highly educated—educated their daughters in the 19th and early 20th centuries. In some families, then, wives and mothers, too, were educated, and this became particularly so within those families that espoused social reform (see Sarkar and Sarkar 2007: Introduction). Most elite women, however, even if they were educated, were still usually secluded at home, until the time that the Independence Movement summoned them out in great numbers. During that movement, "women from elite families who were dissatisfied with the acceptable roles for women took advantage of the opportunities that were available in this period of social change" (Agnew 1979: ix). Many of these women hoped for more social change than what transpired.

The self-identities of women in the freedom struggle could be proud ones. A woman could form a resolve of action, solidarity, and often sacrifice, whether on the ramparts or within the home, and become imbued with an idealism that helped structure her sense of self and her goals for her future and that of her family. Although women "joined the political movement with the approval of their families, not as an act of rebellion against the predominant gender ideology" (Forbes 1996: 134), they could be fierce in their activism. Lilavati Munshi provides an example (Forbes 135: 151; Katzenstein 1978). Born in 1899, she was already a widow with a small child before she was fully grown up. She was then able to continue her education in a boarding school in Panchgani—doubtless with the full approval and necessary support of her parents. In 1926 she married K. M. Munshi, a widower. Both had children from their earlier marriages. These actions clearly stamped her and her new husband, and her natal family as well, as part of the reform-minded elite. A leader in Gandhi's female ranks along with Sarojini Naidu during the Salt Satyagraha of 1930, she later headed a number of Congress committees and important government and nongovernmental posts in Bombay. She was a fearless orator in the cause of women's rights. She was an educated woman, whose famous Brahmin husband was a reformer, a proponent of widow remarriage, an educator, and a writer.[2] These high-level associations through marriage and background, as well as her own talents and accomplishments, provided her with critical activist protections, which later became public service credentials.

The inspiration that a woman like this provided to others continued to reverberate, even when the struggle was through and women were expected to return home. The desire to be out in public, doing admirable things, remained alive in the minds of young women, particularly those whose families were part of the educated elites, and those who had reason to know about the accomplishments of their forebears.

The accomplished women of the immediate post-Independence period, however, were far more exceptional than they might have been, had there not been tremendous drawbacks affecting the possible hopes of others. With qualifications that could allow them careers in government administration and professions such as medicine and teaching, a few women were poised to fulfill some of the promises of their foremothers, those admired figures of struggle who flourished during the freedom movement. But only a very small number of these women, born just before Independence and educated in the ethos of the reform movement, were actually able even to reach toward these hopes, and even fewer to fulfill them. Yet, the reverberations from the freedom struggle continued among women too young to have been part of the political movement. These echoes took the form, in the minds of some young women of elite families, of an urge to be educated so as to be equipped for useful work in the public arena. I refer herein regard to their hopes, as I understand them, not just to be engaged in political or social activism itself, nor

---

[2] He became a leading Congress conservative in the immediate post-Independence government, an ally with Patel and others in seeking a restoration of the Somnath temple, a gesture antithetical to secularism. I do not consider the activism and feminist stances his wife displayed as being defined by his ideology. There is little information with which to characterize her ideas post-Independence; her positions on women's rights, however, located her within the vanguard of her time. It is as a noted social example that I include her in this section.

to seek public versus private employment, but more widely, to their idealistic professional hopes in many fields. These were aspirations not just for jobs and careers as such, but for fuller lives of service and action and self-expression than could be found only at home, lives that not only required higher education, but then also put it to good use beyond the confines of the home.

The stories of women with great hopes and many challenges are legion (Kumar 1993, Liddle and Joshi 1986, Waldrop 2012). Liddle and Joshi offer the story of Reeta, born in 1928, who was kept at home after finishing convent school. Her highly educated father was categorically opposed to higher education for his daughter. But inspired by her mother's sister, who had studied at home, and had "'married out of caste, worked with Gandhi, gone to jail, lived in an ashram, … I took on my aunt's values, [and] I knew I had to have education'" (1986: 76). The ideals of freedom movement women continued as a legacy in this way, conveyed from one generation to the next, most particularly within certain families. Reeta struggled against her father, and with the restrained support of her mother got to university, where she came first in her class. She was then married to a college-educated man who wanted a graduate as a wife, but expected her to stay at home. She separated, got her Ph.D., divorced, and began teaching. "[H]er economic independence … allowed her to make the break a permanent one" (1986: 103), and she was able to support herself and her two sons. Her struggle was at least a dual one, against father and husband, and there were undoubtedly other professional obstacles along the way. But we only have a chance to hear her career story because she was exceptional—because she succeeded.

Friends of mine remember early years that reverberated with after-effects of the freedom struggle, leaving identity impacts, both positive and negative, on the rest of their lives. One whom I will call Hema was born in 1938. I first met her in 1966 when she was a young mother with a one-year old son. We visited in her narrow house in the heart of the old city of Baroda (now Vadodara) near one of the royal gates. We sat around in a tiny room where the family slept each night, rolling up the bedding each morning and putting it into a closet. The houses in that section were only as wide as a beam hewn from a single tree. She and her husband now live in a spacious house in a housing society in one of the neighborhoods that have added to the center city in concentric rings.

Hema was brought up in Surat and went to college there. Earning a B.Com. degree in 1959, she got a job with the Gujarat Electricity Board (GEB). The following year, her mother died, and the family moved back to Baroda, their home town. Her father took early retirement, and Hema obtained a transfer to the GEB office in Baroda. She married at age 26: "Without a mother, I got married later," she said. Her husband had university qualifications and was well employed at age 31. Hema continued her career after marriage, and only quit her employment when her first child was born. She stayed home to raise him and his younger brother while they were small. After both were in school, she took up agency work for an insurance company, which she could do partly from home. She found potential clients through civic club circles, and would invite them over to her house to discuss and finalize their insurance policies.

The Independence Movement had impacted this family's educational attainments. Hema's father was born in 1902 into a Baroda family. The princely state of Baroda was home to reformers and activists, some of them inspired by Aurobindo Ghosh, who was an administrator in the royal court there, with a turn toward radical nationalism, before becoming a mystic and moving to Pondicherry (now Puducherry). Hema's father had finished his SSC and had just started college at the Maharaja Sayajirao University, when he left to join with Gandhi's satyagraha in the middle of his first year. This was at the time of the notorious British massacre of peacefully protesting Indians in Amritsar in 1919, following the nationwide hartal that had been called by Gandhi and accepted by the Congress leadership. In 1920, Gandhi initiated the even more far-reaching Non-Cooperation Movement, one part of which was to ask students to leave college in protest. Many students were caught up in the fervor of this movement, and Gandhi's call to boycott schools and colleges included women as well as men.

Hema's father later earned a certificate in engineering and joined a company in Surat. He was 21 and her mother 18 when they married in 1923. Hema's mother had left school by age 14, though she had wanted to continue. "My mother and father both had to leave studies," Hema told me, not offering reasons for her mother's leaving. However, her mother had been born in 1905, and so the year she was 14 was that same tumultuous year, 1919.

Young people continued to leave schools and colleges in favor of political action throughout the 1920s and 1930s. But members of this particular family settled down in the 1920s to pursue education. Hema's mother's younger sister completed upper-secondary school, while the youngest sister became the first woman college graduate in their Bania caste-group, about 1929. Hema admired this aunt's achievement. Though her mother and father had been educationally left behind during the upheavals of 1919–1920, she displayed great pride in the sacrifice her father (and by implication, her mother, too) had made for the cause. Her parents later made up for their educational deficits through their children. They had four living children (the first of five had died in infancy). A daughter was born in 1936, Hema was the second, and two sons followed. The eldest daughter became a doctor, and the two sons became engineers.

Hema was economically active from college graduation up to retirement age, with a few years' break for her two children. She first did field office work with the government board to ensure the payment of electricity sales taxes, a job which required frequent travel throughout the state, and she later worked as a licensed insurance agent, mainly from home. Her economic contribution in helping support her family was both self-directed and highly effective. One achievement was sending her two sons out of the center city to a private high school in a richer neighborhood. "The atmosphere (in our neighborhood) was not good. I got them both admitted there because I wanted discipline." Her income helped to make the boys' private education possible. "I allocated my time and got much work. I took a loan from the Life Insurance Corporation and built a house. It took years to get a plot in a cooperative society." The address plate on that house has her name on it.

Family members have never suggested that the educational and career accomplishments of their female relatives of Hema's generation were unwelcome to their elders. The family possessed several dimensions of elite status, even at a very modest economic level, and belonged to a progressive princely state. They were upper-caste, urban people. Being a college entrant, even without finishing, meant that her father was within the educational elite, a status then almost exclusively upper-caste. Yet, within these elite status categories, and even in the framework of the progressive polity of princely Baroda, women such as Hema and her sister were exceptional in their own generation. Women born before Independence and reaching adulthood afterwards, while some went to college, have become career women only in a very narrow band of the population. More who might have followed suit were kept from doing so.

Looking at the census data from 1961 helps us in understanding the accomplishments of a woman like Hema, who graduated from college in 1959 and worked in professional roles thereafter, with a break for her children's earliest years. As of the 1961 Census, fourteen years after Indian independence, only 2.9 percent of all urban women, or slightly more than one million, were educated, even to the level of finishing upper-secondary school. Only 223,000 urban women nationwide were educated to the diploma or degree level. Work participation rates of these same women were even more modest. Some 21.5 percent of women with qualifications from high school completion up, or about 220,000 women, were in the workforce; 85 percent of these worked in service sector jobs. Only about 36,350 urban women in the entire nation both had university degrees, and were also employed, as of 1961.[3] During her service for a government board, both in the office and traveling around the state, Hema would count as one of these few. Her later contract work for the life insurance company, though equally professional, would probably have been categorized differently, since it was conducted from home.

---

[3] From Nath 1965: In the 1961 Census only 2.9 percent of urban women were educated to matriculate level or above, a category which totalled 1.02 million. Urban women of this category included 49,000 with diplomas, 128,000 with degrees, 39,000 with teaching degrees, and 7,300 with medical training. The work participation of urban women by level of education was 24.4 percent with nontechnical diplomas, 28.4 percent with university degrees, 62.5 percent with technical diplomas, and 17 percent with technical degrees. For matriculates and above, the joint rate was 21.5 percent. The distribution of urban women workers who were matriculates and above working in services was 85.44 percent.

Chanana's provocative 1996 study of Punjabi women in Delhi, for which the field work was done in 1986, showed changes regarding the valuing and the attainment of college education between two generations of women coming from the same families. A third generation was also briefly considered. The first, called in the study the "Mother" group, were born between 1900 and 1928, and the second, called the "Daughter" group, between 1929 and 1955. They had different educational profiles. These were all urban upper-caste Punjabi families with at least some educated male members. In the first generation, very few women were educated, and a "positive attitude of mothers towards their daughters' education was helpful but not sufficient to allow them access to schooling if men were opposed to it" (Chanana 1996: 124). However, following the persuasion of some of the mothers, and the permission that clearly must have been granted by some of the fathers, second generation women were on average both more educated than their mothers and more equal to their spouses in schooling. The third generation, born between about 1956 and 1983, the granddaughters of the first group, were still growing up at the date of Chanana's study. For them, a college degree was considered by their mothers to be an absolute necessity. As the group from the "daughter" generation became mothers themselves, they felt that their own daughters required a college degree as an insurance policy in marriage. Increases in men's education had also had an effect, because educated men expected to be able to marry educated women.

We can presume that the third group, who would (as of 2014) be between 31 and 58, has more education on average than their own mothers; and we can surely surmise that their fathers agreed to this. There is no career information in Chanana's study, but in an important historical context, an intergenerational change in thinking about gender roles is showcased. Historical experience had a crucial effect, as the second group had experienced the family-splitting cataclysm of the Partition of India in 1947. The women of that second group wanted "insurance" for their daughters, because of the thinning out of the support group around each family that they had experienced, and because of the perceived need for women to be able to support themselves and their families in cases of emergency. The issue of

Partition and family separation is thus very important in Chanana's study. Waldrop (2012) similarly provides, in even greater detail, the narrative of a three-generation family that went through dire circumstances during Partition. In this Delhi family, whom Waldrop calls the Kapoors, the grandmother was born in 1908. This woman became the leading force within her family because her husband was nearly undone by the effects of events of this period.

The interviews Waldrop conducted revealed the terrifying story of the murder of the senior woman's father-in-law in the new Pakistan, followed by her husband's arranging a flight from Pakistan for other relatives of his. These were all people of means and accomplishment; the husband himself was a prominent doctor. But major affairs of the family came under this woman's own management when the need arose. She had been college-educated, as were her female descendants; but the meaning of being educated changed over time, and as one generation of women was replaced by a second and a third. Waldrop's goal in the paper is to locate factors in their lives, and in the larger historical context, that led to greater or lesser female agency for them. She finds that while Partition's effects were playing out, the crisis played a critical role in increasing the agency of the eldest woman. The second generation woman in this family has had much less personal agency than the first, while the third generation woman (who is entering her 40s) now has a great deal.

There is a fascinating similarity between my friend Hema's account of her own agency, including her role in financing and building a house for her family in Baroda in the 1970s, and the recounting by the Kapoor matriarch (born 30 years earlier) of her own role in the building of a house in Delhi in 1954.

> During the building process, I came here at 8 am every morning with food and a flask and sat down in the car to supervise the work.... We decided, however, to rent out the whole house.... I needed the money for my children's education, so I had to rent out. (Waldrop 2012: 619)

In both cases, these elite women stepped forward to play an effective role in helping manage affairs (and build houses) for their families, rather than just caring for them from within the confines of the home while retaining the dignity of seclusion. Agency and effectiveness in assuming some of the management of family affairs, in both cases, followed upon historic upheavals in the wider environment, which thrust these women into positions as partial protectors and/or providers. In each case, a particular loss or crisis catapulted the woman into a different life than she might have had. In Mrs Kapoor's case, the trauma experienced by her husband had this effect; in Hema's case, the loss of her mother, and the determination of her father to restore to his family occupational opportunities that had been interrupted by political upheaval, changed her situation and placed her in a more independent position. In neither case, it is important to note, was the woman in any way operating outside the orbit of what her family needed of her.

The Kapoor matriarch's daughter-in-law, born in 1946, has had much less power in the family, though she worked in the early years of her marriage. But, as she told the author (Waldrop 2012: 623), "I have given my children liberty and freedom, as I have never been given liberty and freedom." She formed an inner resolve to do so, because she saw that not having these opportunities had reduced her satisfaction with her life. Waldrop believes that this woman "sees her own lack of accomplishments from the perspective of the gender norms of the women's movement," which took off in the late 1970s, a decade after her marriage (Waldrop 2012: 627). Hema, eight years older, would not say the same, since she managed to accomplish much in her time without making reference to the women's movement; her drive for accomplishment had more to do with the pressures of the Independence Movement on her family, and the openings it also provided.

Chanana, in her three-generation study, challenged assuming direct links between education and autonomy. "Education may," she wrote (Chanana 1996: 109), "in fact, be better understood as an instrument for status production." She observed that more highly educated women married later, and had more potential opportunities for employment than others; but these factors did not affect their lives very much, because their potential opportunities were bypassed, and they did not seek employment. Women's education changed gender relations among the Daughter group very little, not producing greater autonomy or freedom. Though it raised their ages at marriage, helped them get educated husbands, and affected their points of view, none of these changes greatly altered their position in the family, or allowed for many of them to move into careers. The study was done in Delhi, thus seen as being quite conservative in what even relatively elite women could expect to accomplish as late as the 1980s. This limitation might have been altered if there had been a severe crisis affecting the immediate well-being of one of the families. After all, higher education was granted to upper-caste women precisely as a hedge against crisis.

Some decades later, Delhi has been offering more options to similarly elite, educated women, the same class of women who, in large part, did not work during the 1980s. The granddaughter in the Kapoor family story, born in 1974 and married in 2000, began a modeling career that she has since leveraged into an independent and successful fashion business. She has financial independence, a career, and decision-making power in the family. Her husband has his own business as well. They have two children and live independently near the family home which the grandmother had constructed. This privileged and highly advantaged woman finds satisfaction in her freedom, income, and influence. Earning her own money well in excess of basic family needs makes a big difference in the kind of self-identity she claims in comparison to her mother.

There have been numerous anthropological studies of how kinship structures have limited women and yet been seen by them as supportive in ways that cannot be questioned. In a study in Rajasthan done about 1988, for example, Palriwala (1996) observed women being very conservative in the choices they exercised, respectful of patriarchal authority, not holding on to even their limited rights to family property. Her sympathetic analysis was that this pattern was due to their sense of an urgent need to undergird and strengthen networks that did indeed constrain them and yet also supported them. A rich literature on kinship structures and gender relations, which reports on feminist research that views women's constrained realities with great sympathy (Dube 2001; Ganesh 2001, 2005; Krishnaraj, Sudarshan, and Shariff 1998; Palriwala 1994, 1996;

Patel 2006), brings to mind Sen's phrase "what people have reason to value" guiding the determinations they make. People have good reason to value their support structures. One's compliance with what is arranged by others is carried out, believing this will ensure one's own comfort and safety, whether it turns out to do so or not. Bitterly, it often does not.

Firmly held structures of gender relations are part of an arsenal of family and group survival strategies. Gender in India has been tightly tied to caste endogamy, within-caste marriages arranged and conducted according to caste rules and supported by sacred traditions. Village and lineage group exogamy and caste endogamy are standard in North Indian male-dominated kinship systems, spreading into many parts and castes of the South, as well. Alternate systems that are less heavily male-dominated operate in parts of the South and elsewhere, and in particular castes, tribes, and communities, but these still tend to have lineage and/or family heads who are male. Mandatory marriage is a logical consequence of caste endogamy (Chakravarti 2003).

Families which hew closely to their caste identities cannot allow their children either to remain unmarried, or to choose to marry outside the caste. Lineage heads act as managers for the group, deploying the human resources within the group to the ends of providing for the welfare of the whole, without particular regard for individuals as such. Family leaders have more say, more rights, and more freedom than others. Their authority is accepted because group survival strategies continue to provide benefits, not only throughout rural areas but also among a majority of urban strata. This remains true in a period of rapid fertility decline, as families sharply reduce their completed family size goals to a standard of two children. Reproduction remains a family group affair, subject to group rules and needs; its purpose is to produce new people who can help maintain the group in various ways. The number of children that families optimally need has shrunk to very few. Neither are numerous sons needed, nor, in some areas, any daughters needed; what is required for reproductive purposes are other people's daughters (Kaur 2008).

Modernization theory is an oversimplified way of seeing how emerging alternatives to these systems come into being. As summarized by Amin,

> Modernization theories suggest that new norms, such as exercise of greater choice in marriage as opposed to arranged marriages, and a preference for nuclear as opposed to extended living arrangements, arise after structural change, to bring about change in marriage. (Amin 2006)

This schematic formulation displays a serious lack of specification regarding how the processes of decision-making about marriage come to be altered.

If young women begin to have some new norms, and a partial sense of deciding some matters for themselves, a certain level of authority transfer will already have occurred to allow this to happen. If daughters are to become valued people within their natal families, rather than merely pawns in a strict marital exchange system, their parents have to allow them to fulfill some personal career goals. Many parents have actively urged their daughters to do so from their earliest days. Many of the independent-minded young women of today seem to be the product of parents who changed their family goals a generation ago, sometimes under intense pressures of economic and social necessity. Rapid fertility decline in recent decades has been one response to such pressures. Although its malign outcome of increasing sex selection is widely publicized, in some cases the very goal of smaller families has benefitted daughters.

Looking at influences on gender change brings us to examine the history of Indian women's movements in their first and second waves. The women's movement evolved rather slowly at first, from the early 20th century up through the Independence (Kumar 1993), until a breakthrough event in 1974 brought forth a new surge of feminist protest and activism. Women galvanized by the publication of the groundbreaking report, *Towards Equality*,[4] were of several age groups and represented at least two distinct generations. Many were

---

[4] The title given to the Report of the Committee on the Status of Women in India, Ministry of Education and Social Welfare, Government of India, 1974.

also members of that small, select group of highly educated professionals working in government and academia. Here, the flow of influences on educated women's subjectivity becomes more complex. It is tautological to point out that the members of the newly invigorated women's movement have been activists in behalf of greater equality for women with men. Yet some of the leaders of this second-wave women's movement have refused to call themselves feminists, seeing that term as being tantamount to westernization, so that nationalism has played a strong part in their message; an ironic one, if seen in terms of Chatterjee's (1989) critique. Yet staying strictly within nationalist norms (given the various definitions of those norms found within their particular families), while also becoming professional women, has posed tense challenges in identity-creation for many younger women.

Until the most recent decade or so, most ordinary urban people were rather distant from the women's movement, even if urban people were more exposed to it than rural people were.[5] Many urban women, by contrast, were caught up in labor movements in the cities, and educated urban women served as leaders within some of them (Everett and Savara 1993). Starting in about 1981, the development of Women's and Gender Studies increasingly became a steady stream of influence available to many educated women (Banerjee 2011: 44). Ray (1999), in distinguishing the movements that have impacted women in two cities (Kolkata and Mumbai) up to the early 1990s, has tellingly reported that, in fact, many of Mumbai's feminist activists have worked in Women's Studies departments.

A halting and uneven process of generational succession has prevailed in relation to women's hoped-for careers. Educated women like Hema, born between about 1935 and the late 1940s, economically active in the 1960s and onward, retired by about 2010. They are now part of the generation of the grandmothers and great-grandmothers of young women coming of age today. What happened to women who were young in the 1980s, daughters of that older generation?

---

[5] In 19th and 20th century villages, upper-caste and clean-caste women had hardly even heard of the women's movement, though the social reform movement did reach them through preachers and community leaders. See Shah 2002.

In interviewing girls born between 1988 and 1996, I met some of their mothers. These mothers, who themselves were young in the 1980s, are economically inactive women in direct accordance with my research design. Out of the same generation, however, outstanding career women and leaders of the women's movement arose. There is an incisive disconnect among educated women in this period. Women's movement people themselves have been some of the most impressive career women of the 1980s and 1990s, and many continue their activities today; while most urban, educated women of the same generation have remained quiet and compliant and at home.

The mothers of my interviewees, born between approximately 1960 and 1980, were coming of age as 18-year-olds between 1978 and 1998. During those years, while there was some advancement in the employment of educated women, it was small in magnitude. Several of the mothers I met were college-educated and articulate, wanting to explain to me why they had never taken up the careers that their qualifications might have made feasible. In one city, I came to know a Ph.D. student in her 20s called Tanika.[6] When I went to her home, I met her 48-year old mother (born 1965). She had gotten married at age 21 when her parents told her a match had been arranged for her, though she was still in college at the time. She then completed an M.A. in political science, with her husband's encouragement.

In our visit, Tanika's mother was outgoing, not at all shy, but she said she does not go out alone; she has safety and security concerns about doing so. Her husband chimed in and said that with her education, she could either teach or work in the family business, in which he is giving her training in case of family need, due to any future decline in his own health. She was pleasantly agreeable about this idea, but she helps care for the young children who live in the joint family house together, and enjoys helping to feed and encourage her own two children, both of whom are in university and still living at home. Her husband had encouraged her to continue her education early in the marriage, and is asking her to take business-related training currently, as a form of insurance for the family in case of need. Even today, from his perspective, it would be a fine

---

[6] This is a pseudonym. My research subjects' names have all been altered

thing were she to take up a job. But having not done so earlier, she resists doing so unless later circumstances demand it.

Tanika's mother is one example among middle-aged women I met during this research, as well as among women of various ages whom I knew in the past, whose self-identity as a mother, provider of companionship, and helper and homemaker to her family has been paramount to her above all others. During recent years, while that identity has continued to predominate, educated mothers have not wanted the same one for their daughters. They have hoped that both local and national conditions, and the attitudes within their kin networks, would change to allow their daughters to go farther out into the world than they were able to go. In this hope they are now joined by mothers with much less education themselves.

While the women in this generation of mothers were just becoming young adults, the 1990s brought the onrush of greater globalization and neo-liberalization that had been presaged in the 1980s, but had not been so strong then as it became later. In spite of significant global effects impinging on India in the 1990s, however, for most educated urban women traditional norms of staying at home after marriage largely prevailed. Though the1990s are known as the beginning of an economic boom for India, the range of employment options was quite limited. And as the economy opened further to the global market, although some new occupations indeed became available to women, these were numerically very small in relation to the potential educated female workforce.

Urban female work participation stayed remarkably low. All-India urban female work participation was 6.68 percent in 1971, growing only to 9.19 percent two decades later in 1991. It remained less than 12 percent in 2001 (Government of India 2011). Though some growth in female participation is visible here, these proportions are still very small. The idea of a boom is rather misleading. Urban women's employment in India during the 1990s cannot be called a "boom" in female employment either by international standards or in relation to India's population as a whole.

But, in a countervailing tendency, women's literacy (not broken down by either education level or urban/rural residence) grew from 22.94 percent in 1971 to 39.42 percent in 1991. These decadal rates of growth still appeared slow, and a 1991 study estimated that at this rate, it would take until 2054 for women's literacy to rise to 100 percent (Jejeebhoy 1991). However, by 2001 female literacy had reached 54.2 percent, and by 2011, it reached 65.5 percent. At this rate of improvement, by 2034 it may reach 100 percent, 20 years earlier than predicted in 1991—or even sooner, if the gender gap continues to lessen faster every decade, as it has been doing. We examine increases in women's educational attainment in greater detail in the next chapter, and discuss the paradox these pose for women's career development prospects. For despite improvement in their education levels, women's employment increases have lagged far behind.

The sheer numerical insignificance of educated urban women's employment in recent decades is very marked, when viewed in relation to the size of the female population. (Though most female workers are found in rural areas, with participation rates higher than urban, much less of this is educated employment.) The year 2001 can be used as a marker for what urban women had—or had not—attained in terms of educated employment over the course of the 1990s, just as we used the Census of 1961 to indicate these trends in women's condition in the period preceding that census year.

Employment in the organized sector is tracked by the Ministry of Statistics (Table 2.1). The label "organized sector" refers to regular jobs, also known as those belonging to the formal as opposed to the informal sector. (Though India's informal sector is vast, overwhelming the formal one in size, we are not considering it here.) The organized sector's makeup, when women are compared with men, displays an interesting but troubling trend in employment between 1991 and 2001. Women's rates and numbers grew, while those of men stagnated and even slightly declined. Looking at women, although we see some growth in their numbers, their absolute magnitude remains very small. Slightly less than five million women are shown working in the organized sector by 2001: about a fifth of the numbers of men.

Table 2.1
Employment in the organized sector, India

	Employed in Millions	Percent Men	Percent Women	No. of Men in Millions	No. of Women in Millions	Women to Men Ratio
1991	26,730	85.9	14.1	22,961	3,769	0.1641
2001	27,789	82.2	17.8	22,843	4,946	0.2165
Change	1,059	−4	4	−119	1,178	0.0524

Source: Government of India, Ministry of Statistics and Programme Implementation, 2011.

In what is called the "tertiary" sector, we find many of the workers who are educated professionals (see Table 2.2). The tertiary sector includes education, services, trade, commerce, transport, storage, and communication. It is evident that women have increased their participation in this sector. In the 2001 Census, there were 2,491,211 urban, college-educated women classed as "main workers." Women's share of employment in the tertiary sector steadily grew during the forty years since 1961.

Table 2.2
Work participation, female urban population of India (Age 7+), total and tertiary

	Workers' Share of Total A	Tertiary Workers' Share of Workers B	Tertiary Workers' Share of Total A×B
1971	6.68%	9.40%	0.63%
1981	8.31%	9.40%	0.78%
1991	9.19%	10.80%	0.99%
2001	11.88%	15.20%	1.81%

Sources: Government of India, Ministry of Labour and Employment, 2011; Premi 2006: 249.

Table 2.3 shows a time series of labor force participation rates (LFPRs) of urban graduates, compiled by the National Sample Survey Office for the years 1983 to 2008. These data show a dip for both males and females in 1999–2000, suggesting once again that the end of the century was not a moment of booming employment for either. Over time, the relative rates of participation between men and women are shown to have changed very little. This tracks very poorly with the more rapid spread of female higher education, examined closely in the next chapter.

Table 2.3
LFPRs in India for urban graduates and above, by sex

Year	Male	Female
1983	87.37	35.29
1987–1988	86.40	37.70
1993–1994	86.20	35.50
1999–2000	85.40	30.20
2005–2006	85.90	37.75
2007–2008	85.70	35.40

Source: Government of India, Ministry of Statistics and Programme Implementation, 2011: 54.

In 1961, as we saw earlier, there were only a few thousand women workers who were educated professionals; by 2001 there were almost two and half million. Yet this number is a sheer drop in the bucket, compared to what might have been expected to develop in career opportunities for educated women over those 40 years. Some 36,350 urban educated employed women, compared to the total 1961 population of India of 439 million, made up less than one hundredth of a percent. The 2.5 million such women in 2001, as a share of India's 1,029 million population, were two-tenths of a percent, showing some growth in the tiny ratio over the forty years. But in those decades, the Indian population grew by 43 percent, while during that same time period, the urban, educated, employed female population grew by only 1.5 percent.

How many educated urban women were there, as the 20th century drew to a close, from which to draw this urban educated female workforce? The 2001 Census tells us that there were 9,491,760 urban women who were graduates and above, while there were 16,017,880 men of the same description. Women were thus 37 percent of the total population of urban graduates, men the remaining 63 percent. The share of female urban graduates in professional jobs, however, was much smaller than 37 percent. Shares of the workforce in the tertiary sector, as we have already shown, were five to one in favor of men.

The earliest generation of post-Independence women had a very small share of professional opportunities, but it might have been expected that the next generation or two would have gained a much larger one proportionally. In light of the various historical and social contexts in which women's career hopes have been caught up, it is worthwhile to comment on the commonly found tendency to highlight mainly culture, nationalism, kinship, and social structure in constraining women's work participation and forcing their identities. Much of the constraint, I would argue, has been significantly caused by low overall levels of female education (though these are improving), coupled with halting levels of educated employment development in urban locations, especially in terms of hiring equity for women.

But to this, we must add a serious lack of security as a factor coloring the environment for women attempting to go out and work. The pervasive threat of violence against women—what must be called, in fact, a culture of violence toward women—has maintained an atmosphere of fear and danger for those who venture out into the public space. The hazardous nature of employment has not deterred those women whose families absolutely require their earnings from working outside the home. Up until recently, though, this threatening environment has been a deterrent to many middle-class families from encouraging such a thing, unless, of course, crisis situations require women's participation, or unless the family is from the still very limited stratum of the highly educated elite. Thus, families have been constrained by two major factors, among others: the lack of employment opportunities in which educated women can be hired, and the lack of safety from the chances of violence and abuse.

This brief look at the highly constrained employment opportunities for educated women during the 20th century, even as those opportunities continued to grow piecemeal, allows us to examine educated women's employment trends during the beginning of the present century. We shall examine the kinds of careers that contemporary college women, just now coming of age, are hoping for and working toward, and attempt to explain why this surge in their aspirations is now occurring.

As the educated middle class now grows larger, and some women's roles expand, it is noted that many educated career women cling to being very traditionally correct in their behavior (Radhakrishnan 2011). I too have observed a kind of cultural correctness among my research subjects, zealously seeking to please their families, performing many traditional obligations even as they also embrace some roles that are new. But as I have experienced it, their heads are unbowed, and their minds and hearts roam freely. Young women are seeking new self-identities, hoping to combine work and family in a mixture that can make them contributors, and are trying to prepare themselves for meaningful, interesting and sometimes very new careers. They sometimes hold lofty and idealistic notions of professionalism about what they hope and plan to do. They differ in this way from the majority of female college graduates of the preceding generation, while they are more similar to their (immensely fewer) foremothers who forged a path into careers.

What can we say, then, of the history of women's career aspirations and hopes over time? There were educated women who held professional hopes and who attained some of them, three, four, and even five generations ago. And by so doing, they laid a path of possibility for their descendants and for others who knew about them. There were many others who did not attain nearly as much independence and self-fulfillment as an educated woman might have wished, but who held on to the career idea for younger people. There is a kind of genealogy of ambition to be traced here.

Urban educated women of each generation that I have known over the years have continued to hope for changes that can benefit women, advocating for more education for their daughters and granddaughters and looking forward to more opportunities, greater safety and security, and more self-fulfillment and economic independence for the younger generation. This is most outstandingly true of those who lead the women's movement, a movement which has never died though its leaders have sometimes become disheartened, and which has surged into increased militancy today over all of the issues surrounding violence against women.

3

Gender and Demography: Paradoxical Effects

The increase we currently see in young urban women's education levels and rising career aspirations has a great deal to do with the demographic transition, a process relentlessly taking place all over the world. In India, in just the four decades between 1971 and 2011, total fertility rates fell by almost four children per woman, from 6.5 to 2.6. During this same short period, women's life expectancy at birth gained 15 years; that of men gained 12. In the 1970s, men and women's life expectancies at birth were 44 and 43, respectively, slightly favoring male survival. By 2011, life expectancy at birth had increased to almost 66 for men, and leapfrogged beyond that to over 68 for women.

Life expectancies at birth are highly representative of levels of infant and early child mortality. The great reduction in young-age mortality rates overall has produced a situation where many women now have fewer births than earlier, largely because of their families' increased confidence in children's chances of survival. Adult survival, too, however, has improved so much as to be remarkable, especially when we are able to either share or imagine the memories and life experiences of older people still alive now.

The perusal of the overall population record—both male and female—can be useful for a sharper focus on women's history. From the time the Census of India began in 1872 up through the 1950s, the historical record is one of the appalling levels of mortality. India's mortality was simply abysmal even as it began slowly improving in the 20th century. Then, in the latter half of that century, it improved with amazing speed and effect. To see the sheer scale of mortality and fertility over time, a brief overview will suffice (Table 3.1). So much death and such high-compensating fertility are sobering to contemplate.[1]

Table 3.1
Historical vital rates for India

| Decade | *Life Expectancy at Birth* | | *TFR Per Woman* | *Annual Growth %* |
	Male	*Female*		
1891–1901	21.9	22.9	5.78	0.11
1901–1911	25.0	25.0	5.77	0.56
1911–1921	21.5	21.5	5.75	– 0.03
1921–1931	29.4	30.0	5.86	1.04
1931–1941	30.1	29.9	5.98	1.33
1941–1951	31.0	31.4	5.96	1.25
1951–1961	37.4	36.7	6.11	1.96
1961–1971	**44.0**	**43.0**	**6.50**	**2.20**
1971–1981	50.0	49.0	5.40	2.20
1981–1991	55.5	56.0	4.60	2.14
1991–2001	60.8	62.3	3.50	1.93
2001–2011	**65.6**	**68.2**	**2.60**	**1.76**

Sources: Mari Bhat 1989: 93, 100; Dyson 2010: 21; Premi 2006: 39–40; Census of India 2011.
Note: Emphasis added to bracket the period of most enormous and speedy change.

---

[1] My earlier research on several Indian regions made estimated fertility even higher, by adjusting for the excess female mortality at birth which census sex ratios indicated. Birth figures ought to include unwanted infants who were killed immediately and never reported as being born, but whose traces showed up in sex ratios. I estimated (in Clark 1989, 1993) that for Bombay Presidency between 1881 and 1931, total fertility rates may have been as high as 7.1. This implied that total mortality was also higher, more than could be captured in any standard life tables.

What is clear about women's lives in the past is that they bore an enormously heavy burden in their bodies and on their health, while terrifyingly being subjected to early death themselves. They produced babies, wanted and unwanted, surviving and not surviving, during the peak years of their lives and survived this burden themselves only in tragically limited numbers. Their vulnerability was acute during crisis years of famine and epidemic. During the early decades of the census, population hardly grew; in one particularly appalling decade it even declined. Women's vulnerable role in biological reproduction was essential to the struggle to maintain the population of their families and communities, and in so doing, to maintain the human resource base needed to permit their families to go on into the future.

After the 1950s, as mortality declined and life expectancy increased, women actually fulfilled more of their potential fertility. As female mortality fell lower, mothers survived longer. As a result, total fertility per woman rose; the decade 1961–1971 saw the highest completed fertility of any period. Then, after 1971, increasing proportions of people began to have fewer children. Between 1971 and 2011, women's life expectancy increased by almost 50 percent and total fertility was cut by more than half.

These two huge trends were yoked together in a remarkable way, as families came to expect more of their children to survive. By the 1990s, annual population growth rates had actually begun to slow down. Mortality today is greatly improved compared to its earlier history, though we are now concerned about the components of mortality affecting women. Excess female child mortality due to disfavoring of daughters, brought about by infanticide or lethal neglect, has been a factor for a very long time (Clark 1993). Since the 1980s, sex-selective abortion has weighed in to provide a very efficient method by which disfavored daughters can be eliminated before birth. Maternal mortality in India has also been immense; at about 560 per 100,000 births in 1990, it was still about 190 in 2013. Infant and child mortality in rural areas and among the poor is still in need of vast improvement.

Besides considering these phenomena, a larger point here is that the mortality levels for both sexes have had, and still have, huge impacts on the system of gender relations. In this sweeping view, oversimplifying the complicated history of these decades, mortality and gender can be seen to be linked in the most basic way. On the largest possible scale, women in the past were required to play their most biologically fundamental roles as wives and mothers, reproducing as prolifically as health would allow. We think of this as being so deeply rooted in culture that we simply overlook the demographic regimes under which people lived. The intensely high prevailing mortality regime predicated a high-fertility regime.

These two "regimes," as the word is used in demography, form an intriguing figure of speech. Building on them, we can call the part of the time series from 1891 to 1961—with life expectancies below 40—a Reign of Death. This Reign of Death was rooted in late colonialism, the struggle to emerge from it and its aftermath, the attendant upheavals, wars, famines, and epidemics, and the lack of many modern medical discoveries until after the 1950s. For people experiencing the unpredictability of members of one's own family surviving, the early to middle years of the 20th century were filled with repeated tragedy. Women bore the residual burden of family maintenance when other supporters of the family died.

Fleshing out the human story behind the well-known lag between mortality decline and fertility decline, especially with numbers as stark and notable as those in India, helps us more sympathetically to comprehend the changing concerns of people over time.

A woman I was fond of in years past, whom I will call Anjana, had lost her husband after just a few years of marriage. This woman was born around 1935, and is no longer living. After her husband's death, she and her widowed mother-in-law lived together for the rest of the older woman's life; and such was the case when I met them. This was a once prominent family living in greatly reduced circumstances that I had known in one of the cities to which I have returned for my current research.

Anjana had no children, but had many nieces and nephews, some of whom were all the more endeared to her by the fact that they had each lost one parent. In what should have been the beginning of their lives together, she and her husband had particularly happy relations with his three sisters and their husbands and children, who were an extended set of his kin, dwelling in different cities. Then, well before I met her, my friend's husband died; the husband of one of his sisters died, leaving his wife and children; another of his sisters died leaving behind her husband and children; and the third sister lost her youngest son. The children in each of the sisters' families were left with losses in their lives which were never completely overcome, and which included, also, the loss of their much-loved uncle, who was filled with merriment and kindness. These deaths took place during the 1960s and 1970s. The children left behind were born between 1940 and the 1950s.

This family's story is not primarily one of mortality in early childhood, it is only so in one instance. Rather, it is of the loss to several of the nuclear units of one key adult. The older woman herself, in the loss of two of her four children in adulthood, one of whom was a daughter and one her only son, as well as in the death of the husband of another of her daughters, experienced seriously challenging and security-endangering losses among her offspring. The children in two of the households were nurtured and raised by the remaining parent alone, supplemented by the frequent attentions of the aunt and the grandmother, who took a great interest in their visits, their progress in school, and their times being together as a larger group. Anjana in later years became a postgraduate-educated professional and supported her two-person household, to the great pride of her mother-in-law, who loved to say of her, clapping her on the shoulder, "She is my son!" She was a surrogate son and a surrogate second parent, a person of great character in times of loss and circumstances of hardship.

Her family circumstances were somewhat similar, though offered here in more detail, to those of other old friends, families of friends, and acquaintances. Many people reading this book will realize that they, too, have heard stories from past years of the ineradicable role of death in influencing the structure of their own families and those of friends and relatives, and in shaping the necessary strategies those families followed. Critical losses had to be made up for by both immediate and extended family members, none of whom was well off in many cases well into the 1980s. Death still plays a role in families today, especially among the vast numbers of the poor. But when considering the population as a whole, it cuts a narrower swath, affecting fewer young families and allowing many to escape its troubles longer.

People who are now in their 70s will have borne, during earlier as well as later periods in their lives, the losses of many people that they once knew across all ages. Many persons born in the 1940s, reaching his or her 30s by the time the 1970s arrived, knew of deaths within the family and wider circle, and had also experienced child mortality at close quarters. Reaching peak childbearing years just then, both men and women would have been highly inclined to favor continuing to having children, and many would as a result end up producing numerous surviving children. The 1970s saw the highest total fertility rates of all the decades since Independence. With a life expectancy at birth of mid-40s, and a total fertility rate of 6.5 children, the vital rates of the 1970s precisely fit the actual experiences of death and loss that many, even most, people had known up to then. Life expectancy had been slowly lengthening, on average, since Independence, but not enough to convince people that their hopes for their own children to grow up and survive them were yet safeguarded.

The Indian government had started promoting the idea of small families rather too early for most people to buy into it. The Family Planning Program was initiated in 1951, earlier than in any other country; but from 1951 to 1961, family planning coverage proved negligible. For the next few years, program implementation became marginally more effective, spreading knowledge of methods of contraception and making supplies available at least in some areas. In terms of fertility reduction, however, its effects were absolutely minimal, not at all at the level that governmental and international nongovernmental sponsors had hoped for. In addition, the program had a manipulative aspect in the setting of quotas for family planning workers to fill. There was, among the elite and from various international advisors, a sense of urgency about lessening the rapid growth of population, coupled with an unexamined lack of respect for the human rights of the poor. This combination unfortunately led to an autocratic crackdown on fertility under the watch of Indira Gandhi.

The brutality of forced sterilizations during her Emergency reign in the mid-1970s cast a dark mirror back into the past, to the even more appalling losses of the 1940s, with world war, famine, the splitting of nations, and the bloodbath of Partition. The 1970s were once again a time of upheaval, with poverty, a nation-splitting war, waves of refugees, a brief dictatorship, and then its overthrow by the electorate as a direct result of the forcing of helpless people to lose their hopes for enough progeny to provide them with assurance.

It was only after this that fertility rates began their decline. Mortality decline occurring first, with fertility decline following after a lag, has been the typical (though not universal) experience of demographic transitions. In India, the lag time was haunted by threats and memories of chaos and disruption and unnatural death. These threats began to lift in some appreciable degree by the late 1970s.[2] The Census of 1981 is the first one to signal that fertility decline was beginning in earnest. Mortality decline owed much to major interventions leading to reductions in infectious and parasitic diseases, including malaria (although there has been backsliding in the control of the latter in recent years), tuberculosis, and smallpox (which was eradicated in the 1970s). Immunization of children, increased access to potable water, and reduction in outbreaks of cholera have all contributed to its decline as well (Dyson 2010), although lack of sanitation contributes to inexcusably high rates of child mortality in rural and poor urban areas. Maternal mortality decline has played a big part in lengthening the life span of adult women; continued reductions in this factor, however, are still urgently needed. Death haunts some of the stories in this book still.

One might assume that it has been increases in female education that explain a large share of the record-breaking reductions in fertility observed over the past 40-plus years. Educational advances cause increases both in female age at marriage and in proportions staying single longer. But though gains in women's educational attainment have occurred, India's fertility transition so far has largely been due to contraception, and especially due to female sterilization. Changes in marriage age have had very little effect. A startlingly large share of the fertility decline has occurred among illiterate women, such that "65 per cent of all fertility decline in India between 1981 and 1991 occurred among women with no education" (Visaria 2006: 69).

---

[2] This statement leaves out of its broad sweep, of course, brutal losses still caused by military and mob violence, displacement, natural disasters, crop failures, and suicide.

In addition, evidence from northwestern states, including Gujarat, shows that "fertility can fall despite relatively high levels of son preference" (2006: 71). But as women's fertility levels continue to decline, related and resulting trends may begin to impact their lives, according to Visaria:

> [W]ith rising levels of female education and other socio-economic developments, some women may find the alternatives to a domestic life of marriage and childbearing increasingly attractive. The proportions of women who are not married by age 25 can be expected to increase. It seems probable that a life that does not revolve around marriage and childbearing may gradually become more socially acceptable, especially in urban areas and parts of the country's south. Moreover, even for the vast majority of women who will still marry and have children, the childbearing phase of life is going to be very much shorter than it has been in the past. (2006: 73)

Yet it is also true that "fertility reduction can take place without other enabling conditions being created that will bring about real changes in gender relations" (Krishnaraj, Sudarshan, and Shariff 1998: 34).

Now that more than forty years have passed after the high-water mark of fertility, seen in the 1971 Census, the idea of small families has become a reality. People want smaller families, they live longer lives, more children live to grow up, and more mothers no longer carry in their frail and mortal bodies so huge and daunting a burden of biological reproduction (Clark 1993). Women have more time in their lives to consider other paths to take, as well as providing family care. With smaller families and better survival as general assumptions, not always borne out but increasingly prevalent, ideas about what a woman is, and what she is meant for, have correspondingly begun to change. Let us think about this in terms of how families have considered their options regarding daughters.

The dark side to India's demographic transition is reflected in the ratio of females to males in the population. The sex ratios of the population of all ages together, female to male, declined since the middle of the 20th century from 946 in 1951 to a low of 930 in 1971. This overall indicator has been slightly improving since 1991. But India's child population has had a worsening sex ratio. The 2001

Census showed a sex ratio of 927 for those aged 0–6 years (girls per 1,000 boys); the 2005–2006 National Family Health Survey (NFHS) showed that this ratio had declined to 921 (NFHS-3: 22; see also Patel 2007, Sekher and Hatti 2009). In the 2011 Census, the child sex ratio declined further to 914.

Overall ratios do not indicate clearly the nature of the survival problem facing daughters. The awareness of a deadly form of daughter discrimination began to be widely comprehended in the 1980s (Miller 1981). The sex ratios of children under seven then began to be regularly measured, more clearly reflecting the lethal effects of a prejudice against daughters. The figures indicate that these discriminatory effects are growing stronger, even up to now (Table 3.2). It is widely evident that many women, including some with high levels of education, now use ultrasound and sex-selective abortion to weed out unwanted daughters in utero. This has lowered child sex ratios, especially in the most conservative northern states. While the survival of females relative to males over all ages put together has been improving since 1991, during the very same period the survival of girls relative to boys under seven has been perversely worsening. The technology involved in making sex-selective abortions possible first became widely available in the 1980s, and sex-selective abortion for getting rid of unwanted daughters has now largely replaced an earlier practice of female infanticide. The ratios now display not only the poorer survival of girl children than boys but also the elimination of female fetuses before birth. Whether it is abortion, infanticide, or daughter neglect that is operating in particular cases, the resulting child sex ratios show an interference with normal female child survival rates, and a manipulated imbalance favoring male children.

Table 3.2
Overall and child sex ratios, India, 1981–2011

	Overall Sex Ratio	*Child Sex Ratio*
1981	934	962
1991	927	945
2001	933	927
2011	940	914

Source: Census of India 2011.

This disfavoring of daughters, during a time of overall fertility decline, relates in part to the importance ascribed to sons as maintainers of parents' long-term needs for security. Families have not yet become so secure that they do not need children for the long term. There is no social provision by the state for people during old age; sons have been traditionally expected to provide for their parents at that time of life. This is only one of a complicated set of reasons why sons have been favored, and why daughters, especially at higher parities, have been considered to be expendable. The old-age security concern is singled out here because, above other factors, it is one that seems to be able to show flexibility regarding whether daughters can contribute to it. We see this in more detail in later chapters. There we will better understand what contributions many young women ardently want to make to their natal families, especially when they are the eldest, or the family is poor, and/or when there are no sons.

Cutting against the evidence of the devaluing of daughters is an opposite tendency that favors them, and has been doing so with increasing force in the past three decades. This can be seen in the rapid increase in education, which in urban areas is now disproportionately benefitting young women. Between 1981 and 2001, while urban male literacy grew by 12.4 percent, female literacy in urban areas jumped by 29.3 percent.[3] The gap between male and female literacy has continued to shrink at every census, and at every survey between censuses. The 2011 Census data show all-India literacy (both urban and rural together) as 82 percent for males and 65 percent for females, a gender gap of 17 points. A reduction in the gap has been going on for at least two decades: the 1991 gap had been 25 points. The overall literacy growth rate, both urban and rural, has been much faster for females than males. From 1991 to 2011, while male literacy grew by 28 percent, female literacy surged ahead by 67 percent.

This educational forward march for young women is one of the most remarkable yet under-remarked phenomena of the past two or three decades. Though this trend has been noted on an international

---

[3] The 2011 breakdown will become available when the Social and Cultural Tables for the 2011 Census are released, which had not occurred when this book was completed. There is often several years' delay in releasing this section.

scale (Grant and Behrman 2010), it has been somewhat understudied in regard to India, where there has been more focus on gender equality that has not yet been achieved, than on gender progress that has.

Consider, for example, the growth in numbers and proportions of women in higher education since the 1970s. Data from the Ministry of Human Resource Development show that national enrollment in higher education in 2010–2011 was 27.5 million. Of the total, boys comprised 56 percent and girls 44 percent. Twelve million girls were in college in India in that year (about two-thirds the total number of college students of both sexes that were then found in the USA). The number of girls had been very rapidly growing in each of the previous ten years. In the 40 years since 1971, the proportion of females more than doubled. Male numbers grew from 1971 to 2011 six times; females increased their absolute number by a factor of seventeen.

The gender gap across all educational levels is shrinking particularly fast in urban areas. Percentages of literate urban people educated to upper secondary school and above have grown significantly. In 2001, 45 percent of male urban literates and 38 percent of female urban literates had either reached or surpassed the important 12th grade benchmark (Premi, 2006). By 2008, almost half of the urban literates aged 20–29 *of both sexes* had attained 11 or more years of schooling—48 percent of males and 46 percent of females (International Institute for Population Sciences, DLHS-3, 2008). This is a near gender parity in schooling.

What is the purpose of education for a girl? In the past, a large share of the female population educated whether to 12th standard, college graduation, or postgraduate degrees, soon afterwards married and became housewives, and did not take on any employment utilizing their qualifications. The purpose of education was to qualify a girl for marriage to a good husband, one who was well-educated, settled, and earning well, so he could support her and their family-to-be. Husbands' support was widely required; for as we saw in Chapter 2, employment and economic opportunities for women had been heavily constrained for decades for both demographic and economic reasons, reinforcing social customs that dictated a domesticated way of life for women in a majority of families.

More families, especially urban ones, are now educating daughters with a view to their having lifelong careers. English-language educated groups, in particular, have long upheld the education of daughters as a key to furthering a middle-class identity, but many have not previously believed that daughters ought to take on lifelong careers, unless forced by family circumstances to do so. In the past two decades, however, with India's rapid economic growth under a globalized neoliberal economic world order, the demands of both class and professionalism have changed. New social groups are attempting to join the middle class, and aspiring to take whatever steps they can to secure a middle-class identity. Urban middle-class family identities have, however, fragmented into different versions, some more enhancing for the flourishing of female career orientations than others. Some families are using the push toward greater wealth and higher status to emphasize the importance of sons. They may limit their daughters, while seeking daughters-in-law with qualifications, but perhaps not too much ambition. Other families are finding their daughters to be a great resource in and of themselves.

There are many parts to this story, involving a dense intermixture of economic, social, and cultural changes. The girls I interviewed were all born between 1988 and 1996, in the very middle of the most rapid phase of the fertility transition to fewer children per woman. I look closely at four particular cities which fit in different ways into the profile of an urbanizing India. It is possible to make a comparison between the two smaller cities, with reputable, well-established old universities (Allahabad and Vadodara), and to make another between the two huge cities, with their innumerable universities and colleges of a wide variety of quality and reputation (Mumbai and Bengaluru). In these comparisons, there are important insights to glean about why there is a growth spurt in young women's opportunities to become educated for careers. These were cities in which I had spent time in the past and witnessed an unfolding path of change, and where I have long-term acquaintances whose experiences contrast to those of the young people of today. The cities and states chosen are not meant to be representative of all the regions of India. There is a rough contrast between western, northern, and southern regions implied, but this is not adequate to provide evidence on India's regional diversity. The young women are not meant to be representative of all college women of middle-class or would-be middle-class backgrounds, either. What the interviews do, however, is to surface some new categories of inquiry that have not previously been sketched out for investigation.

In a general profile of an urbanizing India, there are different levels that these four states represent. The proportion of the population of India that was urban in residence rose from 18 percent in 1961 to 31.2 percent in 2011, fifty years later. In the four states under consideration, Gujarat's 2011 population was 42.6 percent urban, Karnataka's 38.6 percent, Maharashtra's 45.2 percent, and Uttar Pradesh's 22.3 percent. Three of these states are considerably more urbanized than the national percentage, while one is much less so. Urban growth bears witness to vigorous levels of development that have occurred in three states: Gujarat, Karnataka, and Maharashtra; the lack of urban growth seen in Uttar Pradesh reflects its broader situation within the northern belt of less developed states. Even within these parameters, however, we shall see that young women in universities, studying for careers, have much more in common across states than we might have predicted just based on the level of development in their states.

Despite the considerable levels of urbanization these figures show, India is actually urbanizing only moderately fast in an internationally comparative context. Other developing countries are doing so much more precipitously. India's urbanization is not made up of suddenly more massive inflows from rural areas; it is the accretion of decades that has created the larger proportions we see. Many people living outside the cities now commute into them, rather than moving there, due to better roads and to upgraded private as well as public transportation, for those whose urban wages can support it. From the vantage point of the small research institute where I stayed about 10 km outside Vadodara, I saw many rural-to-urban commuters daily going by on the road into town. As well as transport by bicycle and bus, as in earlier years, there were more motor scooters, vehicles that have widely spread into the villages, each carrying two or three commuters, and expanded taxi-rickshaws which carry eight to twelve people into town for 10 rupees a head.

Much of the growth in urban population is also due to natural increase, and to the steady arrival of women (an in-migrant stream which has long been known), mainly as a function of their marriages (Dyson 2010). But it is the changing character of urban life that is increasingly relevant to a consideration of changes in gender relations. Young women who grow up in cities, or who move to cities, are different from rural girls, and from urban women of a generation ago. Their educational makeup is different, and their occupational makeup is, too. These differences may not always remain so extreme—but for now, they are very marked.

We have already noted differences in education by gender in India overall. We will now look at the educational situation more closely in relation to particular locations. As background to an examination of one-on-one inquiries in four cities, I consider some recent indicators of the well-being and education of women both nationally and in these particular states. Focusing on the urban districts surrounding the four cities in which the research subjects are located, we look at female literacy and its increase, first in relation to male literacy and then in its paradoxical contrast with the sex ratios (see Table 3.3). We see a gender gap in literacy favoring males in each case. However, the increase in literacy since the previous census gives a different picture. A remarkable improvement in female literacy shows up across all the four states. The rates of literacy increase for males are low; but those for females are much higher.

Uttar Pradesh has a lower level of literacy than the other states, especially for women; the rate of literacy growth for men is high, but its female component is growing even faster. Gujarat's literacy is high, and its female portion is growing extremely fast. Karnataka's women are closing their gap rapidly as well. Maharashtra's trend is smaller, but that state started from the highest level. It has achieved the highest female literacy of any in the group. (Rate increases shrink down to single-digit levels only for Mumbai and Bangalore, which have the highest rates of female literacy in the table, and have therefore had less room to grow.) In India as a whole, women's rate of literacy improvement is 20 percent faster than men's over just the ten years between 2001 and 2011.

Table 3.3
Girls and women: Survival and education, Census 2011

| | *Population Size,* | *F/M Sex* | *F/M* | *Literacy Age 7+* | | *Rate of Increase in Literacy over 2001* | |
	Millions	*Ratio*	*CSR*	*Male*	*Female*	*Male*	*Female*
India	1210.193	940	914	82.1	65.5	7.4	20.3
Gujarat	53.175	918	886	87.2	70.7	9.5	22.4
Vadodara Dist.	4.158	934	894	87.6	74.4	9.4	22.5
Karnataka	61.131	968	943	82.9	68.1	8.8	19.8
Bangalore Dist.	9.589	908	941	91.8	84.8	4.4	9.5
Maharashtra	112.373	899	883	89.8	75.4	4.5	12.6
Mumbai Dist.	12.479	838	874	90.5	86.0	0.3	5.7
Uttar Pradesh	199.581	908	899	79.2	59.3	15.4	18.6
Allahabad Dist.	1.117	902	902	85	62.7	9.1	16.3

Note: Urban *district* data are shown here. The 2011 urban population totals more narrowly defined were, in millions: Vadodara 1.8, Bangalore 8.5, Mumbai 12.5, Allahabad 1.1. All data are from Census of India 2011. Bangalore's name had not yet been changed in this census.

All of this is over and against the performance of the sex ratios, both overall and for children alone, which show unnecessarily poor survival chances for females in almost every urban area and every state shown. The exception here is that Karnataka's child sex ratio of 943 is about equal to the natural sex ratio at birth, and its adult sex ratio of 968 is higher. The natural ratio has been shown internationally to be between 1050 and 1060 boys born for every thousand girls born; or, when calculated as it is done in Indian censuses and survey reports, between 943 and 952 girls born per every thousand boys.

In Bangalore and Mumbai, however, it is worth noticing that the 2011 child sex ratios are better than the corresponding overall sex ratios. This difference can be missed in current discussions of the national decline of sex ratios among young children (as they appeared in Table 3.2). Child sex ratios, female to male, have been going down in these cities, just as they have elsewhere. But in these two major metropolises, the child ratios are not as low as overall ratios; the overall ratios for these locations have actually gone up between 2001 and 2011. An overall ratio comprises the survival results of mortality over all ages, during all the historical years those ages encompass. A child sex ratio encompasses only ages zero through six, and just the last six years of historical experience. It could be going down while the overall ratio goes up, due to slightly better survival for females over age six in the last few years before the census. But if the child sex ratio shows up as better than the overall ratio, it can be confidently expected that the overall ratio will improve the next time around. These observations are suggestive of a need to look at child mortality in particular localities at closer time intervals than census years only, in order to investigate emerging trends in female life chances, and in the life-and-death weighing of the value of daughters to their families.

Looking at the same four states, we now turn to an examination of education trends utilizing data on enrollment in school and higher education available from recent surveys, referring to both urban and rural young people (see Tables 3.4 and 3.5). In Table 3.4, based on the surveys NFHS-1 and NFHS-2, 1993 and 1999 figures show proportions of rural and urban females aged 11–14 attending school in the states in which our chosen cities are located.

Table 3.4

School attendance by state and residence for females aged 11–14, in percent

	Rural			Urban		
State	*1993*	*1999*	*Change*	*1993*	*1999*	*Change*
Gujarat	57.9	54.8	–3.1	78.4	76.5	–1.9
Karnataka	46.4	60.7	14.3	72.5	82.9	10.4
Maharashtra	56.2	78.3	22.1	85.1	89.9	4.8
Uttar Pradesh	38.2	57.1	18.9	68.4	80.0	11.6
India	47.9	61.6	13.7	75.7	82.8	7.1

Source: Dyson, Cassen, and Visaria 2004: 136–137, using data from NFHS-1 and NFHS-2.

Table 3.5
Percentages of youth being educated, 2010

	Age 6+ in Grades 1–12		Age 18–23 in Higher Ed.	
	Male	*Female*	*Male*	*Female*
India	77.1	76.1	20.8	17.9
Gujarat	76.3	70.9	23.5	18.8
Karnataka	78.6	77.8	26.6	24.3
Maharashtra	83.4	80.9	30.7	24.2
Uttar Pradesh	69.4	70.4	15.2	17.4

Sources: National Institute of Public Cooperation and Child Development 2010; Government of India, Ministry of Human Resource Development, 2011.

From the highest to the lowest, Maharashtra in 1999 had 89.9 percent of its urban girls enrolled, Karnataka 82.9 percent, and Uttar Pradesh 80 percent, all representing important increases over 1993, while Gujarat had the lowest percentage, 76.5 percent, which represented a decline.[4] These figures contrasted with those from 1993, showing an increase over the 1990s in enrollment of urban girls in all the states mentioned with the exception of Gujarat. North-south dimensions of difference appear, the southern state of Karnataka holding the lead in the increase.

In most states, families were responding to the economic impetus of the 1990s by sending more of their girl children to school. What was the usefulness of ·their doing so? Recently, under powerfully altered economic and social circumstances, in particularly favored regions and urban locations, women's education has begun to play a greater part in altering what have long been prevailing gender systems within families. And these alterations may no longer be in conflict with women's family support structures, as we will discuss further.

In Table 3.5, we see figures representing trends in school attendance from 2010. At that more recent time than Table 3.4 represented, of all girl children aged 6–17 in India, 76 percent were in

---

[4] The NFHSs include students attending both government and private schools. The decline shown in female school attendance in Gujarat is therefore not based on the surveys having left out some categories of schools.

school. Data are for both urban and rural areas, with age ranges different from those examined before as well. For Maharashtra, the 2010 percentage of children in school was 81 percent; for Karnataka 78 percent, for Gujarat 71 percent, and for Uttar Pradesh 70 percent. Maharashtra and Karnataka showed percentages higher than the national average; Gujarat's and Uttar Pradesh's were lower. These data, encompassing not only urban but rural areas as well, line up well against the urban data shown in Table 3.4 for the earlier years.

Adding in a consideration of enrollment in higher education reveals a dynamic perspective. Enrollment percentages for young school children, male and female, run very close to one another; but students in higher education studying for degrees and other credentials show more of a gender gap. For the most part, this gap appears to be as we would expect, with male enrollments exceeding female. And in Maharashtra and Karnataka, the largest proportions of females aged 18–23 are college students, not surprising given the globalized engines of economic growth driving development in those two states. What is unusual, however, is that although Uttar Pradesh's college enrollments are much lower than those in the other states, its gender gaps in enrollment, in both school and higher education, favor girls. Gender progress of this kind in Uttar Pradesh is certainly notable, even unexpected. It is worth discussing in considerably more detail, which we shall do in Chapter 5 when we examine the individual stories of several girls from Uttar Pradesh who are becoming far more educated than their mothers.

I began this chapter with the observation that the transition in mortality and fertility is a process relentlessly occurring across the globe (though areas persist where it has hardly progressed or even stalled). A worldwide education transition, which is improving education rates for females faster than those for males, is taking place in an almost equally relentless fashion. "Why are rates of girls' schooling rising more rapidly than those of boys?" This is one of the important questions put forward in a recent large research project on adolescents and young adults in developing countries (Lloyd 2005: 147). The question is partly addressed in the same study in statements such as these: "Young women and their parents respond to the incentives that surround them" (2005: 268), and "a daughter's enhanced income-earning potential is argued to be a strong rationale for a parent's willingness to postpone marriage" (2005: 438).These findings, however, indicate the need to look more closely at the "why" questions from within the framework of the family.

In its chosen cities, this book attempts to address the following questions at the micro-level of the family. What choices are families making now, and why do these differ from those made in the same families in the past? Have family needs changed under pressures of changed circumstances? Do cultural shifts more closely reflect new desires or new pressures? Are new possibilities creating greater freedom for girls to choose their paths, and for families to support their choices? Are changes in female education and career aspirations primarily about gender relations, or are they actually about larger issues that subsume gender? In the next chapter, we begin with the differences among the cities, finding family change happening within each of them for reasons that vary along a spectrum of explanations.

4

Professional Aspirations and Education in Cities

In this chapter, I examine the universities and colleges being attended by the young women interviewed in four different cities, all of which contain respected universities of note. I attempt to cast light on how the culture and history of these cities and their universities, and the life stories of families living there and of girls going to college there, have intertwined with each other. The chapter examines how the availability of such institutions has affected the options of parents and daughters living in these cities, and how notions of female professionalism have come to roost in these locations. I sketch some of the unique cultural characteristics of each city, and illustrate how certain kinds of universities color the culture embodied by a city. In examining how a process of changing gender identities is facilitated by each city and its universities, I then turn to the stories of some of the students, and reflect on how their views can be used as a window into aspects of these urban cultures.

The Cities and Their University Cultures

Commonalities between the different cities cut across one another. Bengaluru and Vadodara (earlier called Bangalore and Baroda) were each central urban places in two of the largest and most progressive of India's princely states, Mysore and Baroda. Each of these two cities is now a burgeoning hub of economic change. Cutting across that commonality is a different comparison, made up of two different pairs. Vadodara (with a 2011 population of 1.8 million) and Allahabad (1.1 million) are much smaller cities than the other two. In each, a centrally important university has long held sway, and continues to do so. At the other extreme, Mumbai (12.5 million) and Bengaluru (8.5 million) are both highly globalized megacities, with a multiplicity of institutions of higher learning, colleges and universities of every kind and level, and highly reputed research institutes.

Most of the universities I visited are public, government-sponsored institutions, following rules established by the University Grants Commission. They are similar in that respect, which has important common implications for some of my subjects, even though they are found in culturally contrasting regions of India. The character of each university or college and its surrounding city, however, in each case is unique.

Allahabad University is one of India's oldest English-medium universities, founded with the blessings of the British imperial government in 1887. Many of its buildings are in the imperial style of the late 19th century, and its humanities departments make use of these old and unremodeled structures. There is an atmosphere of elegance and decay, yet of tradition and character as well. The law school is housed in newer facilities, yet it, too, has an air of tradition, character, and high standards. The students I interviewed at Allahabad University were either in humanities or law, each one attesting to a sense that she was in luck to be studying at Allahabad University. One had come from Bihar to study law at the Allahabad University, and stated that the Allahabad University and the University of Delhi had the two top law schools in the country.[1] Other students said that this university was one of the top places for people to study who were hoping to join the Indian Administrative Service (IAS).

---

[1] This student, whose mother had a high-level career, is outside the group of subjects selected for the main study of this book. Several interviews in each city turned out to be ineligible; these were only used for information not found otherwise.

The city itself is strongly marked by being a huge military base with a large cantonment area, also very traditional and long-standing. There are colleges in other parts of the city, most of them constituent colleges of the Allahabad University, but the main university is very close to the cantonment. This military presence adds to the atmosphere of settled tradition in this place. The very airport is a military one, only partially fitted out with a domestic service area. The city has parks and museums, the finest of which is the Nehru family's historic home. But as a place in which to live and move about, the city is lacking in facilities appealing to young people. In particular, girls do not sense that they have either freedom or safety to go about very much. Many women students live at home, while others board in an entire enclosed campus of women's hostels. In such an environment, it was not surprising to find students who were serious about studies, yet looked forward to a day when they might be able to live somewhere else.

In Mumbai, my work took place mainly on the SNDT Women's University's Juhu campus. The germ of SNDT began in 1916. This autonomous university for women was founded in Pune by the social reformer D. K. Karve, and later given strong financial support by the head of the wealthy Thakersey family, who named it after his mother. In 1936, its headquarters were moved to Mumbai. As a public university dedicated exclusively to the education of women, it partakes of a memorial atmosphere of heroic struggle in this cause, with displays of large portraits of many great women and a few great men of the late 19th and early 20th centuries. Its buildings are modest and utilitarian. Its faculty includes both men and women, but is predominantly made up of women. Its student population is a very diverse representation of many parts of India and many kinds of backgrounds.

The city of Mumbai all around the quiet grounds of this university's Juhu campus is a bustling place, with plenty of public transport on its busy thoroughfares, places to go out nearby, eateries, amenities, and shops. Most girls commute to classes here from homes and lodgings both near and far away. Mumbai is an enormous, global megacity, but one whose distinct neighborhoods still have a powerful definite character of their own. In this environment, one can find many students who see their future careers developing in this same city, either returning to their varied neighborhoods or taking up work in the city's widely spread commercial sectors. There are also young women from outside the area, living in lodgings while going to college, who hope to find work either in Mumbai or back in the region they come from. The two departments in which I interviewed there were Extension Education and Management.

The SNDT management program is called the Janaki Devi Bajaj Institute of Management Studies. There is a Bajaj institute in downtown Mumbai which ranks first among management institutes in Mumbai, and which is private and expensive; the one at SNDT is ranked third, and is public and inexpensive. Students were impressed with the fact that the prestigious Bajaj name would be part of their qualification. I also had some interviews with girls introduced to me by a lecturer in the Sociology Department of a college affiliated with the University of Mumbai.

Vadodara, often still known by its older name, Baroda, is the third largest city in Gujarat. The railway line and the national highway connecting Delhi and Mumbai pass through this city, which as of 2011 had a population of almost 1.8 million people. It was the central site of the former Maratha Gaekwad dynasty, which in ruling over the princely state of Baroda governed a huge portion of the now unified Gujarat state. The Maharaja Sayajirao University of Baroda is the largest university in Gujarat, and the only one which uses English as its medium of instruction. The germ of the Maharaja Sayajirao University of Baroda was the founding of the Baroda College in 1881 by the Maharaja of Baroda, Sir Sayajirao Gaekwad III. The college later expanded and became a university bearing his name and title in 1949.

The culture of Vadodara and its university are closely tied to one another. As Gujarat's largest as well as its sole English-medium university, Maharaja Sayajirao University provides an island of educational and cultural cosmopolitanism in a conservative state. A remarkable woman of towering reputation, Hansa Mehta, was vice-chancellor of this university from 1948 to 1956. She had earlier been the vice-chancellor of SNDT University.

The daughter of a prime minister (or Diwan) to the Maharaja, she was one of very few girls in Baroda to finish high school and go to college. She went to England, where she formed a bond with Sarojini Naidu and returned to become an activist in the Independence Movement's most militant period. She became president of the All India Women's Conference in 1945 and helped draw up a Charter of Indian Women's Rights. She then became a member of the United Nations Human Rights Commission and, along with Eleanor Roosevelt, helped draft the Universal Declaration of Human Rights, insisting that it should refer to "all human beings," not "all men." She became part of the Constituent Assembly, which drafted the Constitution of India.

A collection of Mehta's writings and speeches, brought out under the title *Indian Women* (1981), has much to say about home science, an academic subject area which she championed and in fact pioneered in India by establishing a Faculty of Home Science at the Maharaja Sayajirao University. Unlike her own brilliant and internationalist life story, her writing on this topic maintained the traditional assumption that most college-trained women's potential roles would be as housewives with an education. Of course, at the time that she became Maharaja Sayajirao University's vice-chancellor, as she herself noted, only 2 percent out of India's 200 million women were literate (1981: 33). In her writing, however, she also made allusions to the impetus that home science as a field might eventually have for women's careers.

I interviewed several career-minded postgraduate students in what was formerly the Faculty of Home Science at Maharaja Sayajirao University, now called the Faculty of Family and Community Sciences. These young women are working on new research topics in areas that hold potential to provide professional identities for them in the current era. I also interviewed students in the Department of Museology in the Faculty of Arts, who planned on museum careers.

Baroda had been one of only five princely states deemed large enough and grand enough to merit a 21-gun salute under the British; and Mysore was another. The Gaekwad Maharaja of Baroda and the Wodeyar Maharaja of Mysore were both seen as golden examples within the British system of indirect rule, heralded as progressive, modern, reform-minded rulers after being carefully groomed for office under British tutelage. Just as the Baroda Maharaja had been instrumental in planting the seeds of the university that bears his name, the Mysore ruler established the University of Mysore in 1916. The Central College of Bangalore, formerly part of the Madras University, became a decentralized part of this new university under the aegis of the princely state.

Bengaluru is the fastest growing city in India, whose population of only 800,000 in 1951 had grown to 8.5 million as of 2011. It is India's fifth largest city; the momentum of its industrial and commercial growth being unequalled in the country. In the past 25 years, Bengaluru has emerged as a major center for international outsourcing. Its success in attracting software and IT-enabled service businesses has caused it to be regarded as the Silicon Valley of India. The United Nations Human Development Report of 2001 recognized it as one of the leading global hubs of technological innovation.

It was not within the University of Bengaluru that we did research for our earlier study (Clark and Sekher 2007). Instead, we interviewed some young women who were attending Institute of Finance and International Management (IFIM), a private postgraduate business school located in the high-tech surroundings at one edge of the now-enormous city. This is a private institution, modern and sleek, located next to the campus of the famous Infosys Corporation. As a private B-School, it is expensive, and the students I met there had either to have their own resources, or to take out significant loans to attend. The fact of this institution's existence is not discontinuous, however, from the background of Bengaluru as part of the princely state of Mysore. It was under a remarkable administrator during royal rule that Bengaluru first became deeply invested in science and technology (Heitzman 2005). It is as a science and technology magnet that this city has become a hotbed of enterprise and business education.

The Sample

The sample of career-minded college girls, which forms the cornerstone of this study, is highly unrepresentative, except in some rather particular requirements. Starting by contacting professors in each city that I either knew or was introduced to, I requested that they recommend students who, in their opinion, were committed to having virtually lifelong careers, but whose mothers had not. This led me to interview young women who were undergraduates or postgraduates on the campuses of universities and colleges mentioned in Allahabad, Mumbai, and Vadodara during my 2013–2014 research stay. These were supplemented by interviews from Bengaluru from my 2005 research. Most of my interviewees did meet my qualification of having mothers who did not work. In the midst of interviewing them, I learned that this criterion was not met in some cases (as is noted when needed).

By way of providing more intimate cultural outlines of the cities and universities under consideration, I here attempt to derive some notions about those cultural outlines from the interviews themselves. The view is restricted to a necessarily narrow focus in regards to culture by concentrating persistently on the gender relations uncovered within the sample. While continuing to insist that this sample is meant to be neither an ethnography nor a scientific representation regarding gender relations in these cities and universities, I allow some leeway for what it does reveal. In this chapter, focused on the geography of education and professionalism, I also begin the process of telling the stories of my research subjects, a process which anchors this book.

There are several types of stories which illustrate the issues in gender relations being brought to consciousness and confronted by young women studying in these four cities. One type of story illuminates the steep gradient between rural life and an educated profession, through the eyes of a young woman planning on her own initiative, against her father's wishes, to devote her life to a career. A second type of story is about young women (and sometimes their whole families) who are coming from other cities and towns in order that they may study in these cities. A third theme within stories is about what career-seeking girls believe that their future in-laws may or may not allow them to do in the years ahead, and how the particular city affects this perception.

The spectrum of professions desired by the career-oriented young women I met was novel and diverse, even surprisingly so. The careers they aspire to range from fashion designer to philosophy professor to rural manager, and from advocate to ergonomic kitchen planner, and also include teacher, corporate social responsibility officer, researcher on tribal textiles, marketing or finance director, museum curator, and IAS officer. The fact that such a wide range of careers is being imagined and planned for by young women studying in universities today will be analyzed in more detail later in the book; but for now, this fact simply stands out as a vivid marker of change from the past. No longer is women's career education targeted almost exclusively on teaching and government employment. Nor is a college education still oriented mainly around preparing women for a higher level of homemaking. Many factors have loosened up the range of career possibilities girls can consider and for which they can obtain professional training. I focus closely on the within-family factors contributing to this expansion, without losing sight of broader and more multidimensional contexts. I ask, too, what the idea of professionalism means to young women who are actively seeking to become professionals.

A Village Background

There were 36 young women, each studying at a college or university in one of the four cities, who met my interview requirement of their having noncareer mothers.[2] Only three of these emerged directly from a village background, one that presents special hurdles for a young woman to overcome. Other girls had families with village roots that lay further in the past: some of these families still owned rural land operated by relatives. But a girl coming by herself from the village to the city to study at a university faced family challenges that daughters of migrant families did not. Rita provided an example of this.

---

[2] Others are used in supplemental ways when relevant.

Rita, in Allahabad. Rita's parents live in a village in Uttar Pradesh (UP), where her father is a farmer. She has had a rigorous climb out of this background, and is nearly independent already. She was 20 and in her first year of the MBA program in the Rural Development Program of the Allahabad University when we met there. She comes from a caste within the other backward classes (OBC) category.[3] She began,

> I belong to a small village in Kanpur District, with no facilities. I want to develop villages further.

> I went by bicycle to a school six kilometers away. After finishing intermediate, I went to Kanpur. I took a room on rent with a classmate and spent three years there. My parents were opposed, especially my father, though my mother was more cooperative. I did tuitions for pocket money.

> I have an elder sister and a younger brother. I'm in the middle. My sister is a teacher. My mother convinced my father, and he took loans for the girls' education. After I have a job I'll pay it back. My father is 50 and studied up to 12th standard. My mother is 45 and is a graduate with BA in political science. She had wanted a job, but my father and grandparents were zamindars of our place, so she did not work. Zamindars hold a strong position in society. My mother's father, who was a subdistrict lawyer, was impressed with that in arranging her marriage.

The educational contrast between the mother and the father sharply stood out, underlining discrepancies among the circumstances of the three children.

> When I was born my parents were disappointed I was a girl. I was neglected, so I became this way, very determined. My older sister's dreams are not as big as mine. She can compromise with her career and with her life. She is 25, and our parents are planning to marry her next year. My younger brother can have our 14 acres of land and rent

---

[3] I accepted answers given to my question, "What is your caste?" without pressuring for further specificity, finding that many girls preferred general categories, and that some were not aware of more specific ones. This did not apply to their parents, when I was able to meet them.

it out. I don't think my father enjoys his work. My brother wants to have a different career.

Considerable family tension was encapsulated in the awkward situation of the mother, an educated woman married to a less-educated man: a woman who had wanted a career and instead, at the behest of a well-educated father, became a landowner's wife living in a village. The arrangement of a marriage for a college-educated daughter with a noncollege-educated man marked caste and status behavior in relation to gender, particularly, of the earlier generation of parents. The inner conflicts that Rita's ambitions occasioned in the mother could well be imagined. The girl's sense of having been unwanted cast a poignant light over the struggles of a mother trying to fit into the stereotyped expectations of the family culture into which she had married. It was interesting to learn of the older sister's holding less ambition for herself, yet sturdily facilitating her younger sister's aims and accomplishments.

> When I got top rank in 12th class, my father decided more education was okay. I got admission in a college in Kanpur and my sister helped me move there. For two years, I lived with a classmate, and my last year there I lived with my sister. Then she came with me to Allahabad for my application and interview for this postgraduate program. My father was quite opposed. So I left home again, went to a hostel and said, "Okay, I'll do a job and next year I will go to the MBA program with my own savings." I stayed one week and they relented. I had gotten this tough admission.

Her proud defiance was visibly strong. So were her appreciations for her sister, and her resolve not to submit to her parents in the matter of marriage.

> Four years after getting a job is the first time I'd be willing to get married. My MBA is a two-year program, and then my brother still needs educational support from me. He is 14, in 10th class, and needs six or seven years more education, up to B.Tech. I will marry whom I want to marry—it is the most important decision of one's life.

She has an understanding with a young man who is willing to wait all those years for her. He and his parents are just the kind of family she would like to live with. She intends to tell her family of her decision once she is financially independent, and not until then. But even in her resolve to have the career she chooses, and to earn her own way and to marry whom she chooses, she is still intent on helping her brother along. Within the community her family belongs to, she says, she would not be able to do this openly after marriage. Her loyalty to her younger brother keeps her from being open with her parents, though it is they who will benefit from their son's becoming educated.

She lives in a hostel at her institute, and has applied for a scholarship; this year, she is studying on loan. "I am preparing myself as a development professional. There are jobs both in NGOs and in the government sector, such as the NRHM, the national rural health mission. After some years, I plan to open my own NGO for women empowerment."

Rita, like most of my research subjects, was introduced to me by a professor who respects her academic achievements and has resolute hopes for her future. One senses that it would be a source of great pride for such professors to see their protégées succeed despite the obstacles.

Coming from Far Away

Metro cities are liberating, and are deliberately chosen by some young women as places to go and study. Some girls travel on their own initiative to a school far away, leaving their families behind. In other cases, families have moved from one place to another, at least in part for their children's education so that they will have better chances in the future. The stories in this section illustrate young women seeking professional training opportunities by moving on their own far away from their native homes. We then encounter families who have moved as a whole in the next section.

Shyamili, in Bengaluru. Shyamili had moved from Jharkhand, and was studying for her MBA-equivalency at IFIM in Bengaluru. She was 23, and had earned a B.Sc. in physics with honors from a college near her home in Jharkhand. She had missed two years of education after graduation, because the family had needed her at home. Her brother was now in a college near home pursuing a B.Com. degree, and her sister, with a B.A. in sociology, was teaching primary school in Kolkata. Both parents had finished only 10th standard. Her mother was a housewife, and her father had a confectionary shop. The family was in the general category of caste classification, as she reported it (no specifics were mentioned).

Shyamili had taken a loan, on her own, to study for her management degree. She said she would take five years to pay it back, either before or partly after marriage. After she gets her MBA-equivalency, she said, she would like to have an arranged marriage, because she trusts her parents' judgment. She insisted, however, that she would work in Bengaluru, and that the boy she marries should be there, too, holding a good job in a company, with either an engineering degree or an MBA. She has confidence that her parents, even from far away, can find this kind of match for her, and will cooperate with her conditions. "I need a boy both in and from Bangalore so I can have my in-laws' help. If not, my husband will be there to assist me." She would put off having a child until after age 28, and says that one child would be enough.

Although her parents have only middle secondary educations, and live in a less-developed region, some eliteness of social status must be assumed for this family if Shyamili is to be proved right in her expectations of what kind of marriage they can arrange for her. There is an educational disjuncture between the parents and their children, but socially, in order for her to have this confidence, they must possess recognized standing among educated people who travel to distant cities for work. In other words, although Shyamili is from far away, she seems to be from a social status layer with people to whom distance matters less than her place of origin alone would suggest. Bengaluru is a magnet city for young people coming from such families.

Kusum, in Vadodara. Kusum, who is 22 and comes from Kolkata, was introduced to me by a professor in the Museology Department in the Faculty of Fine Arts at Maharaja Sayajirao University. She wants to become a museum curator. She has been at the university for four years, living in a women's hostel for arts students; she did her B.A. in archaeology, and has finished the first year of her M.A. program in museology. She became interested in archaeology during high school. She did an Internet search and found that Maharaja Sayajirao University has a highly rated department. Back home, she had attended a private school. She is from a Gujarati Brahmin family living in Kolkata.

Her father, age 50 and 12th standard educated, left the family when Kusum was 3. Her mother is 43, also finished 12th standard, and stays home. "My father's younger brother is supporting us. We are a joint family with aunts, uncles, and cousins—18–20 people in the house. I have one younger brother, who is 19 and in his 2nd year for Chartered Accountancy."

> My family is supportive of my studies and career plans. In high school I began studying science and engineering, but then found I didn't want to be an engineer. As I shifted, my family said, "Do what you like. First finish your basic qualifications, and then work and help out." But they are only partly depending on me; it is my return favor to them.

> The Masters is basic. I will first try for a job with one Masters. Sometimes museum jobs require a double Masters, with either conservation or history. I would choose conservation. I will look for jobs anywhere and everywhere; they are not so easily available.

She expects to get married, but not soon.

> My family says, "If you like a guy, tell us. If he's stable and of good family, we will support your choice." My mother said she'll get me married by 28. My requirements are that he be truthful, trustworthy and stable, and have a sense of humor. I am willing to live with his family. I have no thoughts about kids, except that I'd like to adopt one. I will work till retirement. Taking a child break depends on how well my husband is supporting us, so I can spend time with the child. Both husband and wife should be responsible for the care of the home, and take turns cooking.

If it's a government job, it will be mostly 9 to 5, and private museums have similar hours. It would be good for both spouses to have similar professions, or the same one. Husband and wife should decide together how to spend money. If he transfers, first I'll analyze the situation. Who needs me the most then, and what is the period of the transfer? Then I'll come to a conclusion.

What is professionalism, I ask her?

It means that you should be good in the work you're doing. I should attach myself to the museum, talk to others, and learn as I go along. Every day I am learning new things. Objects have meaning. I see differently than I did five months ago.

Kusum is from a comfortable background, despite the lack of her own father. Like Rita and Shyamili, she has a lot more education than her parents. She imagines a future with a husband who is involved in the professional field that fascinates her. But she also hopes he can support her and the family if she takes a break for a child. This may be less likely with two museum salaries than if her husband has a more lucrative career. Her career destiny is not necessarily very urban. Museums are in many remote locations, and she says she is willing to go wherever the jobs are. She is only 22, and there's no pressure to marry until she is 28. Just how it might all work out is not clear, but there is no sense of stark necessity in her story, which is filled with an unshadowed delight in learning. There is a lack of an urgent practical sense of what would be sustainable in seeking joint careers with a husband. This makes her story unlike those of several girls we shall meet in the next chapter.

Sonam, in Mumbai. Sonam was introduced to me by a management professor at SNDT in Mumbai. She had lived in Kolkata earlier in her life, but more recently hails from Nagpur, where her family now lives. She earned a B.Tech. degree from Nagpur University. She had obtained an engineering job in biotechnology there, but was more interested in managing. "I had a job in my hand, but I preferred to go for further studies." She says the corporate sector in Mumbai is good for internship opportunities. She is 24 and in her final year for the M.M.S.

Her father is in business and her mother is a housewife. Her younger sister, aged 20, works in radio.

> I am looking for Human Resources and training. I want to be a trainer, and need to know the full range of training that an organization needs. Later, I will open my own training and placement agency. Training is about developing skills, both technical and nontechnical. I am more interested in the nontechnical skills, which are important for personality development.

Sonam has a dynamic personality, and is a student leader among her peers in the institute. She is Marwari, and originally from Rajasthan. Her fiancé is Maharashtrian, and lives and works in a town near Nagpur. She is enthusiastic about becoming part of his culture, and she meets no opposition from her parents. She wants to find work either in Nagpur or in the nearby town where her fiancé is a manager in a bank. He plans to start his own manufacturing business. His parents are deceased; they left him land and a house. She tells me that she wants to work with him as a partner, and she envisions her training consultancy as being part of the same business as his manufacturing concern. For a few years they each need to be employees, but they have this joint ambition.

> For sure I'll work after marriage. I'll take a break after about three years for kids. We want two kids plus one adopted, both sexes. I want to send all three to good schools. He wants his maternal aunt and her husband to come and live with us; they live in a village now. I love her! There are advantages: someone to talk to, and mutual support. When children come, it will be good having these relatives live there.

What does professionalism mean?

> It means being honest and loyal, managing your personal life well. Having dedication for your work; being hard-working. We should not mix personal and professional life. I am the head of a team here. While working with my husband as a partner, it should be the same: don't bring work and its problems home. My mother has told me since my school days, forget work while at home, or plan about it for half an hour, then leave it. I work for recognition. My boyfriend works for money.

This young woman is not only dynamic and effervescent, but also shrewd and practical. Her finding a man with an ambitious plan and some resources to work with seems to attest to that. Reaching out to his relatives to be part of the family that will live together is a way to create the home support base that many girls are looking for. Her freedom to cross cultural lines and choose where to live and whom to live with are impressive. Of course, Nagpur is also where her parents and sister live, and they will also be a support network for her. They are a migrant business family already. Her ambition is to be a woman in business, gaining personal recognition while she bills clients and earns income. While it is difficult to guess how well all of this will work out for her, at present she appears to be blazing a trail of her own choosing.

What the In-laws Will Allow

Some girls were experiencing, as both a present and future concern, the question of what their future in-laws would allow them to do after marriage. To some girls, this appeared not only unknown but also uncontrollable. Not all of my research subjects spoke of this worry, however, because some of them were very certain they could insist on career and get their way.

This topic was the most common gist whenever in polite conversation I was obliged to speak briefly with other people about my research. Either socially or accidentally, I encountered middle-aged middle-class people, all English-speaking, who informed me with great assurance that even college-educated girls' in-laws would not allow them to have careers after marriage. It was not surprising to hear this assumption from people well above the age group of my research subjects. It was at times a concern to hear some male professors of female students speak in this way. However, when I interviewed girls who said they were worried about this question, the actual prospects they saw for their futures appeared to them to be much more mixed, between an open possibility that they might be able to sustain a career, and a reluctant acceptance that they might not be allowed to continue their work.

Abhita, in Vadodara. I was introduced to Abhita in the Faculty of Family and Community Sciences at the Maharaja Sayajirao University of Baroda. She was 23, and had recently earned her M.Sc. in the Department of Clothing and Textiles there. She had been working for the last year as a research assistant in the same department, and was about to begin work toward her Ph.D. Her project is working with natural dyes and fibers, finding out new sources, working on colors and standardization procedures. She travels to meet artisans at different locations in small towns, where natural dyes are more commonly used than in cities. She loves her work.

> I'm not sure if this is a life career or not; it depends on my in-laws. But I love working! The decision is mine about when to marry. If I want to continue with this career, even get a Ph.D., my parents are support-ive. I can continue towards a Ph.D. if I wish, by clearing an exam and an interview. I would need to give a presentation on the project first. I joined my work on a one-year contract and can renew it. My project managers, two professors, like my work. I probably should marry by age 25. But right now, I have time to explore my career.

My colleague doing the introductions for me in this department was surprised to hear that Abhita had some doubts about doing her Ph.D. She felt that this girl qualified as being career-oriented, because her work is very good and the department is keen to keep her. The department is pushing her to get her Ph.D. so that she can join the faculty, and I sensed that my colleague thought that the department would win its bet with Abhita. I was not sure of this.

Abhita's father is 48 and completed 10th standard, and so did her mother, who is 45.

> They live in Baroda, and I live with them. I have an older brother, who is 26 and unmarried. He has his B.Com and has joined with our father's business as a goldsmith wholesaler. We are Soni by caste, and Hindu. Our family is middle class. We have a two-bedroom house; my brother and I sleep in the front. I sometimes contrib-ute money, but it's not usually required. I'm saving my income and buying gold as an investment. My father is handling this. He would give me any amount from it that I ask. I can pay my own fees for further education.

I'm not yet decided on what qualities I would like in a husband. I would like to continue to work, if my in-laws agree. I probably will want children, but I don't know how many. I'd like to live in a joint family after marriage. My brother is likely to bring a wife home soon. Our parents allow a love marriage, but I would prefer arranged, and of the same caste.

I am allowed to go out of town for my profession. I have done this at times, working with artisans who are using natural dyes. My parents understand my enjoyment of this research. They do check to see if I am safe. They don't mind how many days I'm gone or whom I meet. I freely carry money around with me.

It would be good if my husband has a Masters' degree. A small house, maybe three bedrooms, would be fine for me; I am not any more ambitious. My husband should be more ambitious for money than I am. I will say NO to dowry. I'd like to stay on in Baroda, but I would be willing to move with my husband. I'm not sure if my skills will transfer.

When I asked her, "What does professionalism mean to you?" her answer was, "Professionalism means doing what I enjoy as work."

Unlike many other girls I met, Abhita was demure. Though she was impressed with both the career she was already involved in and the approval it had won her, as well as really enjoying the scope of the work itself, she did not take it for granted that she would be allowed to continue. Nor did she insist that she would make this a qualification for her acceptance of a husband and family among whom to spend her life. Yet her parents sounded quite indulgent about her going ahead. If the department is to win its bet on Abhita, with her creative eye and her excellent taste, it will do so with her parents' encouragement, but contingent on their successful search for an equally permissive and encouraging in-law family.

This career possibility after marriage seems to be a change in what a goldsmith's daughter could previously expect. It has much to do, in this particular case, with the escalation in Abhita's education level well beyond that of her parents. It does not relate to their needing her to support them. As a second child with an older brother, Abhita is supported by her parents' pride in her accomplishments, rather than by their need for her to become independent to help them. They do not suggest that she must become dependent and retiring upon marriage. If she does so, it may be because she is not willing to insist and does not marry the sort of partner who supports a career wife. She wants an arranged marriage within her own caste, and this may limit the number of prospects holding those values. There is also a threat to her career if her husband moves his career and family to another location, for then she would have to leave her professional location and network behind. Her specialization is very location-specific, as she is involved in discovering Gujarati village craftspeople using natural dyes that they make from local plants, and the job opportunity she has in hand is in her own department. Her university colleagues would consider her leaving a significant loss, even though they might find a talented replacement researcher.

Rani, in Mumbai. Rani, a young Marwari woman studying at SNDT in Mumbai, had pungent things to say about this topic of being "allowed" to do things. Aged 24, she was in her first of the two years for the M.Sc. in extension education. She already had a B.A. in Arts. Her interview poured out of her without my even asking questions. I got in a few questions now and then. The rest of the time she just had so much she wanted to say that I did not interrupt, though some of her statement conflicted with other parts of it.

She says she is interested in improving the knowledge, attitude, and practice of people with needs, encouraging farmers to use good practices, empowering people, especially rural people, improving skills, working with their felt needs and what they want. She believes in a family approach and in making programs efficient on the cooperative principle. Opportunities with the qualification she is earning include jobs in nongovernmental organizations. "What I want is to serve the community, not just me, and to create a sustainable environment."

> As of now, I would like to work, but this degree is also very important as a backup for crises. If my parents are looking for a guy, he and his parents should give me the freedom to work if I want to. People all ask, 'What is your qualification?' If they ask that about a girl, I say, 'Why not let her work?' Marwari families say, 'We have money; why

is there any need for her to work?' I just want the freedom and the satisfaction! I know I will devote myself wholeheartedly to my work, to my children, to whatever I do.

Her father is in his 50s and has a B.Com. degree.

He used to do painting as an artist, but now has shifted to printing, which is his own business. My mother—I'm not sure if she completed a B.A. She studied to the 14th year and then got married. She is also in her 50s. My older brother was born in 1981, and I was born in 1989. We are treated equally, but my brother can do a few more things. He has his MBA and works in marketing.

I have always wanted to do practical work, not theoretical. If I have the qualification, I would like to be a team leader. Rural work will be fine, with some facilities and a good position. I need to gain experience with how the people do the work, and then rise a bit. Salary, dignity and promotion, all of these are needed. But I'm not really that career-oriented. I may get engaged before this degree. If I get bored, I'll join work. They should not stop me from doing the kind of work I want to do! I want freedom, and this will be a condition I set: freedom to choose.

I prefer love marriage, because then I will know who I'm getting and how he'll react. I will know him well. What if I don't like the person I'm arranged to marry? My parents are okay with love marriage, but they say to avoid other religions. I wouldn't mind another caste. I'm not sure if my family will agree. I want to keep my parents close. They live here; I was born in Rajasthan and brought up here in Mumbai. My parents do support my having a career; they say that if there's a crisis, the wife can help, so gain as much knowledge as you can. I am privileged! My parents are supportive.

I will try managing childcare with my family if I do want to work. I am devoted to my family. They are my support. They are the ones giving me freedom. Because they have respected my thoughts, I'll be glad if I can repay them by understanding their thoughts.

We need to use our degree, or it goes to waste. The first few years are important for establishing yourself in a field. Then you can take a few years off and rejoin. The husband is the one who is going to understand me.

Rani is experiencing a kind of ping-pong game of opposing points of view. She is trying to stay on top of the game, but without clear guidelines. She is passionate in her personality, but not in having a very clear commitment. The longing for the freedom to choose, not to be bound by conservative Marwari customs, but to range about with her interests as she wishes, is strong in her account. The family is not rich, as are some in their community; they have had their challenges. They want Rani to be secure. She wants to use the skills and approaches to community development that she has heard about in her courses, to have an interesting life, and not to be bored.

Priya, in Vadodara. Priya told me a story full of drama, throwing the reputedly progressive culture of Vadodara into high relief as the context for a family undergoing some emotionally very uncomfortable, yet apparently rather urgent, changes in gender expectations. Her family (like Rani's) was also from Rajasthan. They had moved to Vadodara from there about twenty years earlier. I met Priya, who was 25, at Maharaja Sayajirao University at the Faculty of Family and Community Sciences, where she was a postgraduate student in interior design.

Priya said her family, which belongs to the Agrawal community, had moved to Vadodara because this was where her father and his brothers had decided to start a business. There is a family store in town, in which several of her uncles own shares. Priya has a showroom in a section of the store belonging to one of her uncles, which she has designed and where she represents a well-known brand of electronics. She has built a career path toward interior design that includes a previous job with an architect, an interesting current research project on ergonomic kitchen design, the prospect of becoming a lecturer in her Maharaja Sayajirao University department, and the hope of starting a freelance design business as well.

None of this has fully separated her and her future, however, from relatives in Rajasthan, who are now hounding her family. There are three daughters to marry off, two younger than Priya; so the relatives are demanding to know, why is she not married yet? Her younger sisters are studying for degrees as well, and are receiving the same scrutiny from their far-off relatives about when they are going to get married.

Her father is searching for a groom for Priya who will suit her. She describes her father as being very stressed by the conflict between her demands and those of the Rajasthan family, but leaning hard toward her. She wants a husband and in-laws who are in favor of a woman who earns; but this is not the culture that she comes from. She wants to be sure not to move back to the north, but to have a husband located in Vadodara, Ahmedabad, or Mumbai.

The research project Priya is pursuing is particularly interesting. Her plans for designing an ergonomic kitchen, where the people living in a house can comfortably do their own housework if they wish, intrigued me, since it contrasts with traditional older houses that require either the family members or servants to do stoop labor to clean up. An ergonomic kitchen would currently be unaffordable to families that cannot also afford servants, so members who do housework would actually be choosing to do so. Her research on this therefore fits into an urban middle-class lifestyle demand for upgraded housing designs. I. found Priya practical, insightful, and well-prepared for going forward with her work and the career it would lead to. Yet there was the threat from the relatives, who believe that a woman should not work. "We should not eat from a daughter-in-law," they say; and thus, their own daughters who are becoming daughters-in-law should not work. She has much scorn for this position.

This story demonstrates the entwined and conflicted relations that can develop between a particular community's gender expectations and a localized urban culture. It speaks to the changed ambitions regarding gender that can emerge, as an in-migrant family acclimatizes to a new social environment. Coming from a conservative location, this family is partially merging itself with a more cosmopolitan local culture in Vadodara, which permits more freedom to women. Doing so causes much uneasiness to Priya's mother. It is her father who is championing her.

What the in-laws will actually allow, in the currently unknown future, will inevitably affect many of the girls I met, even some who are very assertive. This theme of what in-laws will allow links us to Chapter 5, where we will find assertive girls who, like Priya, are supported by doting and determined fathers. Those fathers are not ready to constrain their girls' desires for lifetime careers after marriage, and their daughters therefore do not worry about other people not allowing them to do and be what they want. Yet, at least one of the stories to be encountered there (that of Vimla) straddles this question, like the story of Priya, because of the insistent demands of the community the family comes from.

In this chapter, it has emerged that all the examples, except that of village-born Rita, are of middle to upper-caste backgrounds, unlike what we shall see in the next chapter. Such caste backgrounds may sometimes seem to smooth the disjuncture between less educated parents and more educated daughters, and to ease the challenge of changing some of the gender mores that have prevailed in the community. What about girls outside the Hindu social hierarchy? I had three girls from other religious communities in my sample, one Christian and two Muslims. They were all very assertive and feisty. They also had very comfortable backgrounds, and parents who were not interfering at all with either their ambitions for careers, or their freedom to move around. The mothers in each case were worried about their marriage prospects; but the father was highly supportive, and the mother was trailing along.

5

Status-raising as a Father–Daughter Project

Rani and Priya are both, in different ways, very suitable lead-ins to this chapter where we consider the role that fathers play in a girl's career ambitions. These two girls from similar backgrounds help to show the difference that parents, especially fathers, can make for their daughters. Rani may not be so likely to get a marital family which is supportive to a lifetime career; her parents may not have that goal for her, and her community is conservative about whether wives should work. Priya's father, though also from a conservative background, is swimming against the tide of his community. His daughter is also farther ahead in a promising career, and he wants her to have what she needs.

The role of fathers is critical in the lives of daughters aiming for careers. When the family is in difficulties, paternal advocacy becomes particularly urgent and sustained. Several stories will illustrate the importance of hardship in setting the stage for a daughter to be groomed for "self-dependence," as some of the interviewees or their families interestingly called it instead of "independence." These are families with pressing needs. In the cases recounted in this chapter, the father is urging the daughter on, and his wife is supportive too. In addition, in most of the cases, the daughter is providing present benefits to her natal family. For contrast, I provide one case in which it seemed that the daughter's career was less important to her family, did not fulfill their needs, and so would not receive their ongoing support. At the end of the chapter, I offer a narrative from a different social location, a privileged one, where it also appears to be the father's project to support and advocate for the daughter's career, though the motivations in that family are quite different from those affecting families with urgent needs.

At the far edge of Allahabad, across the Yamuna River, is a neighborhood with narrow lanes and small houses, rather like a village. There, in an extremely small and meager house, *Jaya* lives with her parents as she has since her birth 17 years ago, along with her two younger sisters "and one sweet little brother." She is in the second year of her B.A. program at Allahabad University, which she had set her sights on attending since was five. Jaya's parents are proud of her—they have discovered that she has the capacity to go far. A few years ago, they did not have high expectations for her that they do now; but when she was 15, she won the National Cadet Corps gold medal. Now they are geared up to see her through to achieving her ambition; she aims to become an IAS officer.

They are poor but proud, humble in their habitation, and firm in their determination. They have the dignity of being OBC in category, village artisan in origin, and of village officialdom in actual occupational background. Jaya's father has a small, unstable, and temporary government post; his own father was a Block Development Officer (BDO). He is college-educated; his wife finished 10th standard. He had wanted to be an advocate, but had to cut short further education to fulfill the needs of his family. He now puts all of his money into his four children's education. There is no possible way he could give Jaya a dowry, he insists; and Jaya's mother vociferously says "No!" to the very idea of giving dowry. They are not apologetic; they look to Jaya to make good, and plan to keep supporting her in every way they can until she can support herself. Then, if she has the ability to help her siblings along, they will accept this from her but no more; she should have all her own money to support herself in the years ahead.

This girl reminds me of a young woman whom I met in Bengaluru a few years ago (Clark and Sekher 2007). *Sarita,* who was 21 at the time of our interview, was from Pondicherry, where her father had a job as a government proofreader. The father was college-educated; the mother was not. They wanted to see their daughter move ahead beyond them. Sarita was eldest of the two daughters, and there were no other children. Her parents had sent her to a good college in another town, and expected her to go on for an M.A. after graduation. They felt that she would be more employable with a further degree. However, before the end of the final year of her B.A. program, she and several of her classmates were recruited by a major multinational corporation to move to Bengaluru as soon as they graduated, to take up BPO (business process outsourcing) jobs. Despite misgivings, the parents agreed, because their daughter would be living together with classmates there, and the pay was outstanding. When Sarita started work, her salary was at the same level as her father's. The family was astonished and excited that she could do so well. Sarita's plan was to complete her M.A. in human resources management by correspondence while working, and then move on to a more professional level career. She would help her younger sister first, and then become independent.

In terms of family structure, *Vimla,* in Allahabad, appears similar. But the ramifications of her circumstances are far more complicated. And her opportunities to pursue her career are very mixed, for quite different reasons. Aged 22 and a D.Phil. candidate, Vimla is the eldest child, surging forward beyond the background of her family. She teaches at the University of Allahabad, where she is researching and planning to write a D.Phil. dissertation that combines feminism, philosophy, and education studies. One of the scholars she most admires is Chandra Talpade Mohanty.

Her family lives in an apartment at the outskirts of Allahabad, two parents with children all in college or university, two daughters and a son (the youngest). The family is entirely supported by Vimla's Junior Research Fellowship of ₹19,200 per month, which will continue for the years it takes to finish her doctoral degree. The family moved to Allahabad from the small town where Vimla went to a college, to which they had first moved from their native village where her father had been a farmer. The father has a college degree; the mother is illiterate. They are proud people, OBC in caste, with land in the village and relatives who send them some produce every year. Some of the relatives are college-educated, others have very little education.

After first moving to the town near the village, the father sold supplies in a shop. Vimla then gained admission in the postgraduate program in Allahabad and moved there, living with a roommate for a year. But her father did not want her to be "alone, a girl in the city." So the following year, her family moved to Allahabad to be with her. The father has sacrificed his employment; he now devotes himself to taking his children to college and bringing them home again. Vimla recently had to go to a northern city for a two-day seminar. Her father went with her for protection. She does not go out anywhere unless he is with her.

She is the support and the linchpin of her family. They are proud of her intellectual accomplishments, and want her to study as much as she wants and to go as high as she can. Her unschooled, illiterate mother is particularly vocal in her admiration and support for her daughter. "I am happy she has a good career. She is famous in our society!" she says, with vigorous gestures.

The contradictions Vimla faces in her situation strike her acutely. She is a well-read feminist, and also a deeply respectful daughter. These are village people who have rejected their village's narrowness and made an exit from a joint family in which instances of violence against women could be witnessed by the children. It was shocking to watch. "This is not the climate I want my children to grow up in," Vimla tells me her father said when he moved them to the nearby town. She speaks with great respect of his action. "My father is a courageous man for my education. He didn't have as much as he wanted of it, and he wanted it for me." She tells me his dream is that she becomes "both a good lady, and an independent lady."

She points out, however, that this double goal seems to contain a contradiction. "How can I improve my personality when I'm told, 'You are a girl, not a boy'?" she says to me (in short, how *can* I become an independent lady?). Her father is extremely protective. He shares some of her decision making with her; but the clothes she is wearing were his choice, not hers. "I wanted short sleeves and no collar," she says, pointing to her kameez; but he insisted it be made with long sleeves and a collar. She exclaims, "My sister wears jeans!" There is more responsibility placed on her, the eldest.

We talk about her future marriage, which she would like to decide for herself but expects will be arranged by her family. She emphasizes that she has no chance, in her situation, to meet anyone! The family will seek someone who is as educated as she, placed at a similarly professional level. "I want to marry a boy who'll respect my opinions. I'll say no forcefully if it's not the right boy. I have no doubt about my decision being right. When my father arranges a meeting with someone, I will spend some months talking with him on all topics. I'll ask him his opinion about me, and about women. He must want a girl's freedom and participation in decision making." The insistent tone she used was rather striking.

I ask her about how her future marital family should be managed.

> With both of us in professions, when it comes to caring for our child, it should be both of us. My aunt and uncle are teachers, and they have two children; another uncle and aunt are caring for them. When family members are available, it's good. I want a joint family, and good in-laws. If there's a problem with childcare, I will leave my job and give first place to family and child. But there are relatives available, and my mother tells me I can call on her for childcare. I hope my husband will allow me to call my own mother. This is not a big problem in my family; childcare is shared.

> I want my mother-in-law to support my career, and my father-in-law to do so, too. While teaching, I can take care of my child after 5 p.m.—a teaching schedule makes this possible. I'll take six months of leave for childbirth, and then return to work. If I'm transferred, I'll ask my husband to move; if he is transferred, I will move. Men are more dominant in this.

> I will be a professor. My career plan is to get my P.G. diploma and my D.Phil., and to continue working from now up to age 65. I love my teaching and my students. My passion is to be a teacher.

Vimla's interview, and her insistence on knowing her own mind and expressing it, reminded me of two girls from Bengaluru (or Bangalore, as it was known when I was there), whom I had met a few years earlier. *Kamayani* was also 22 when we met; she had a B.Com. degree and a job in a BPO company. It was not night work;

she indexed and adjudicated insurance claims from several US insurance companies. She liked her work and was doing well; in fact, she believed she was in line for a promotion, and was excited about that. She wanted to become a manager and take a business visit to the United States.

Kamayani was from an orthodox family, as she herself labeled it; each month she turned her entire salary over to her father. It was being invested for her future; it was not needed by the family. She was not allowed to go out of town with the other young employees for a company retreat. Her mother and older sister were both submissive housewives. Kamayani herself was charmingly persuasive, even somewhat forceful, as she vowed that she would manage to stay attached to the labor force after marriage. She also planned to use her well-honed communication skills in urging her parents to let her marry a boy of her choice. She said, "I would not easily accept a 'No.' I would ask for reasons." Her persuasiveness was somewhat unconvincing in light of the restrictions a traditional in-law family may impose. I suspected that she was being allowed to work for a while after college to amass a savings account managed by her father which could become part of her dowry or marriage settlement. If she were to continue working, that would be up to the marital family.

This was the same position as the one explicitly expressed to me by Vimla's family regarding her freedoms after marriage. The situation was very different, though, in that Vimla's family needed her income, and actively endorsed her increasing professionalism as a result. They expressed great pride in her, as well, rather than simply allowing an interval before marriage to be filled with work, as I judged that Kamayani's family was doing.

Vimla's interview also reminded me of another one I had with a different young woman in Bengaluru. *Revathi* had entered the call center industry at a time of sudden need on the part of her family. Her father had an accident and was unable to work. Although she had a law degree, a job in a call center could provide money quickly and copiously to the family in its difficulties. The conservative expectations of the family were transformed as they learned of, regretfully accepted, and then benefitted from the resourcefulness and earning power of their eldest child. Revathi's own view of herself also changed. What I particularly remembered, while thinking of how firmly I heard Vimla express her view of her own judgment, were these words of Revathi's: "I have confidence in myself. Whatever decision I take is right."

We have now looked at two Allahabad families—those of Jaya and Vimla—who are relying upon their eldest child, a daughter, to rescue them from a reversal or a deep insecurity that the family has met with. We have compared them with two South Indian families whose eldest daughters, Sarita and Revathi, had already begun to carry out such a rescue, and with one (that of Kamayani) where neither was rescue necessary, nor was the girl's career strongly supported. In each case, the role of the father has emerged as crucial. No less crucial does it appear to be in the case of a girl who is set to lift her family up out of an unquestionably working-class background, entirely on her merit.

This is the story of *Vasanti*, the daughter of a milkman from a village in Maharashtra. Vasanti is 23, and in the final year of her Master of Management Studies program at a public university in Mumbai. She intends on a career in marketing and retail management. She spent 14 months working as an assistant marketing officer in a big company in Mumbai after her Bachelors, and before beginning her Masters' program. Having studied in this field, she wanted to make doubly sure that this career path was her true choice. "Would I really like marketing? What are the line activities? I introspected and found that, yes." Her superiors were impressed with her, and promised to recommend her to any company she may choose to apply to after she finishes her Masters this year. "These are people who have seen me work with commitment and dedication," she tells me.

Vasanti lives with her mother and father, her two younger sisters, and her grandmother in a small two-room house in central Mumbai where she grew up. In the family's native Maharashtra village, her father completed the 10th standard and her mother the 8th in Marathi medium schools. "Our village has 45 houses; but 20 of them are shut." Those people, like Vasanti's parents, have migrated to Mumbai.

Vasanti's family is of a caste whose traditional occupation is selling milk. Her uncle still has a dairy in the village and they visit him once a year. When her father was 16, he migrated to Mumbai to work with his older brother selling milk in the city. They collected milk every morning at a big dairy in Worli and delivered it to the customers' homes.

When he came to the city "he saw educated people," she said, and wished he himself could have been more educated. He married when he was 25 and his bride was 18. The next year Vasanti was born, and two more girls followed. "They never regretted not having a son; they've always encouraged us to do everything a boy would do." In a telling statement, she says, "He wants to complete his dreams through me." Now the father is employed in a small firm working as a peon, earning ₹8,500 a month.

Vasanti is more than self-supporting already. She saved for all her postgraduate fees from the year's work as a marketing officer, and contributed money to her parents as well. And she still does. She earns currently by providing tuitions at her home to 17 children who live nearby. Two batches of kids come each evening, from 6 to 7:30 and from 7:30 to 9, sitting with her in the only complete room in the house. The younger sisters study on the balcony, and the older people sit in the kitchen while lessons are going on. Vasanti earns ₹11,500 a month this way. She wants to continue her tutorial service even after she gets a professional job, expanding it with the help of a neighbor; she feels committed to the neighborhood children. Their parents are not much educated, and the kids need this kind of help with their studies.

She is not under pressure to marry soon, nor to have an arranged marriage; she may select her own partner. It's possible she could be married to a boy of her caste, because some of them are also becoming educated now. She says that she has broad-minded parents, but that they come from a narrow-minded village. She does not face restrictions on her movements, and is free to go out of town for exhibitions and school events, and to go out to parties with friends. In future, when she meets a possible marriage partner, she will insist on personal compatibility and a four to five month acquaintance, freely moving around town. The boy should be on his own, earning, from a good family, a non-drinker, and living in Mumbai. He should support her working. She has a particular requirement: it must be understood that 50 percent of her income will always go to her parents. This is clearly stated, in spite of her saying that she would gladly live in a joint family (with his parents). She expects to negotiate these matters directly with her husband-to-be, who will make them clear to his parents.

Vasanti is not the only working-class girl among my interviewees clearly headed for a middle-class career but she is one of the most remarkable. Her father's longings and regrets, as he carries out his family role while doing the job of a peon, are a poignant part of the story. Her parents' unstinting encouragement and lack of restriction form part of the required context. She also has strong advocacy from committed professors, and is a top student. She has translated herself into a global person, too, in her work experience with the company. One has to credit also the forwardness of the city of Mumbai.

Vasanti has ideals about her work and influence in the world. She feels committed to help educate poor children; and she insists that the company she works for must be an ethical one, with good business practices and good management. "You carry the image of your company, and it should bring pride to you," she declares.

"I want her to do what I was never able to do!" We have now heard this remark, or something akin to it, from several fathers, across several different cities and sociocultural locations. In addition, these girls have surprised their parents, who had not previously had expectations that their daughter would make an amazing leap to another level. Education was important, but expectations were modest. But the daughter reached a point of opportunity, and then convinced her parents to let her move ahead. The father's humble job and the mother's lack of education were not keeping them from investing their family's hopes in their daughter; in fact, this humble background seemed to be the very cause for their doing so, when that daughter was their firstborn child. It seemed that they did not regret the firstborn not being a son; it was rather as though it was seen as a special, unique blessing that their first child was a talented, energetic, and an intelligent girl.

A young woman of very modest background who is the eldest child of her parents may become the standard bearer for her entire natal family. The expectations placed upon her tend to grow as her accomplishments grow. She is to succeed and be a source of pride as well as income for her family. In families with no son, the daughter plans to continue to support parents in old age; in families with younger siblings, she intends to help to see them educated. If there is a younger son, the daughter is expected to become self-supporting but not support her parents later on. She is not to expect a dowry; her earning capacity is expected to suffice. These are challenging, sometimes even daunting expectations, yet their burdensomeness is outweighed in the outlook of my subjects by their own transformation into something much bigger within their family circle than what a woman used to be. Another girl in my study, who is the only child of her parents, says, "I am their son."

The vividness of their pride dominates my recollection of our meetings. The way these girls embraced the opportunity to be my research subjects, and aspects of how they wanted to present themselves, made me a temporary instrument in their process of self-identification. Though I was a single listener, it was as if each girl was amplifying her voice for the larger world in speaking to me. All the young women I have reported on in this chapter, and some of those in the previous one, are assertive about what they are demanding.

There were two points at which this assertiveness was vocally underscored in a similar way. My questionnaire included: "Will you continue to work after marriage?" This question elicited a suddenly different facial expression and tone of voice than those the girl had used before, as she answered, "Yes, of course!"—expressing almost scornfully the notion that there could simply be no question about it. My questions about offering dowry or accepting a demand for dowry were similarly answered, in a rather indignant version of the retort, "Of course not!"

The three student subjects of very modest background, Jaya, Vimla, and Vasanti, interviewed in Allahabad and Mumbai, each comes from a family in the SC or OBC categories. They are studying in government colleges, availing themselves of special scholarships and reserved places as allowed by law. These privileges are being utilized in a completely matter-of-fact way, having been part of the law since these girls were infants, or even before that in the case of the youngest one. The ambitions of these families for their daughters reach far beyond the accomplishments of the parents, and this is accepted by the girls and their parents as being unquestionably reasonable. The effect of the girls as they speak is confident and practical.

With regard to bodily habitus, there is a marked difference, however, between Vasanti and Jaya, on the one hand, whose families allow them freedom of movement, and Vimla, on the other, who is so strictly watched. She is the most accomplished of these three, the most aware and well-read regarding issues that face women. Yet she is the most restricted, perhaps due to what may unfortunately be the realistic caste-based concerns of her father. Vimla's community is Yadav, the caste in power in her state (UP), a caste which has a virulently conservative majority. The drama of this family is the split from the village branch of the family, the possibly strife-torn pulling away from them, and the insistence by her parents that their daughter should be allowed and encouraged to be an achiever (and likewise for the second daughter). In order to allow this, the father has to protect them very closely, not just from random strangers, but likely also from members of his own community.

The strain is reflected in Vimla's bodily habitus. The way she usually carries herself is stern and correct. I do not use the real names or keep photographs of my subjects to protect their privacy; but in a photo I saw on campus of Vimla among her classmates, her bearing is remarkable. She has a fierce dignity in her look and manner. In our personal interview, she was gentle and appealing. When we visited her family, though, she was formal, and did not translate for me; a colleague accompanied us. Yet she stated again, in the very presence of her proud and formidable father, that she supports this family now.

The notion I offer here is of assertiveness as a capability (Sen 1999, Nussbaum and Sen 1993). That is, asserting who one is now, and what one wants to do and be, is an act in itself. It is more than having an aspiration or an ambition; it is a statement of the self (Taylor 1989, Bannerji 2001). The conscious self, when asserted and expressed in words, is a kind of moral force field. These women have this moral force in their bodies and in their self-presentation. Their circumstances may or may not allow them to fulfill their ambitions and aspirations, but nothing stops them being able to say, now, who they are and what they plan to be and do. Assertiveness, in this sense, is in itself a capability: a potential that has been actualized in thought and awareness.

That changes in family gender expectations and in female self-identity articulate with one another, not separately, was a core finding stemming from the earlier work in Bengaluru (Clark and Sekher 2007). Questions are answered in different ways under various background circumstances: but the unbroken theme of family embeddedness prevails. Family aspirations for a decent life can call upon daughters just as keenly as upon sons, if not more so. Under the stresses of the present, with economic dislocation and fracturing cultural conditions, these families need to address their situations through new family security strategies. Turning to their daughters to help lift them out of their anxious dilemma, these families place gender identity and its transformation at the very center of the issue.

Gender is located in these new circumstances in a new position of possibility and greatly hoped-for potential. Gendered experiences of various possible kinds of cultural capital to invest in are avid and acute in this class segment. Young women are very aware of the boundary between their family background and their aspirations, and they scale that boundary when they identify instances where they can collect and invest cultural capital, for their own benefit and for that of their families. These instances include urban residence, exposure to a wider world, the aspirations of their households, the unstinting cooperation of their families, the friendship and mentorship of their professors, and the visible existence of professions that interest them. It cannot be omitted, as well, that an infrastructure of social capital has been laid by for these women over decades, in the form of the expansion of educational opportunities and the mainstreaming of gender awareness and redress. Now is the moment when these savings are being drawn upon with zeal and determination by the youngest and newest women of the new, upwardly mobile middle class.

Bourdieu's theory seems to omit the potential for new cultural capital to be formed, or to be created. But during this time of rapid social and economic change, a creative shaping of the cultural clay seems to be facilitated in the hands of particularly capable people. In my finding, Bourdieu's view of a less advantaged person's habitus inevitably restricting her social mobility seems too harsh, as well. The habitus, as a practiced set of class-formed inner tendencies, can be seen as more of a stumbling block, which can be overcome by people who are able to bring it to consciousness and act upon it. This possibility, of course, depends in part on external factors that converge upon a person's life trajectory, affecting her substantive freedoms.

I want now to set the stories of these young women, rising vigorously from straitened circumstances to help their families and themselves, against another case of a strongly motivated girl, showing a father's strong paternal support for his daughter's career plans but for quite different ends. This is the story of a wealthy, well-established family in Allahabad, a city that might seem to be too conservative to sponsor a daughter's ambitions.

Shruti is an affluent upper-middle-class girl. The daughter of a judge, she wants to be a lawyer herself. She is 21 and in the 4th year of the five-year program which the Allahabad University Law College offers, leading to both B.A. and L.L.B. Honors. I first interviewed her at the college. She had earlier studied in a convent school, accounting for her excellent English. Her demeanor is elegant and genteel. The family is Hindu, of Bania caste. Her father was recently elevated to be a judge in the High Court.

Her mother completed a B.Sc. and the first year of an M.Sc. program; but before finishing, she got married and quit. She had moved to Allahabad for marriage, and decided she would not work after that. There are two daughters, no sons. Shruti's younger sister is 18, in her first year of college, and wants to be a writer. The parents are supportive of their daughters doing whatever they want. "I was in Class 5 when I decided on law," Shruti says, "and my father was fine with it. My mother at first wanted me to have an easier career, such as teaching."

She says, "They don't consider a career to be necessary for a girl; but if she's forced to work, she should have qualifications." I ask, "Do they require you to be married?" "They do want me to get married eventually. Getting married is a better choice, they say; staying alone is tough. You need someone to turn to; you need a family." She is not keen to get married, at least not anytime soon. Before she does, she feels that it must become very well-established that she is not "forced" to work, but does so as a personal requirement.

> I may find my own marriage partner; my parents have the final word, but caste is no bar. I would want a boy from a respectable family, well settled, with good qualifications and earning. He *must* allow *me* to work! He can be a businessman or a doctor, it doesn't matter, but one thing I'll make sure of—I will continue my work. I'm passionate about it! Men now agree that girls should work. My in-laws must agree.

> I want to go into litigation. Here we have the High Court, so either Allahabad or Delhi will be a good place for me. My career plan is to pursue being an advocate and practice at High Court or Supreme Court: it will be exciting! I don't want corporate work, or to be an employee. My father has always planned his own schedule. I want that much freedom. I'd be a professional rather than in some corporate firm. I've interned often over the last four years, and met many female lawyers in both Allahabad and Delhi. Litigation has been male-dominated in the past.

One of the reasons she gives for her career choice, as a woman, is to bring more justice to women.

> It suits me to be aggressive. I admire my father and want to do as he did, and to make him proud.

> Some ladies say they wouldn't want a daughter-in-law like this, so getting the right mother-in-law may be a problem. I'd like a joint family; I would enjoy the company. I do enjoy housework, but will need a helping hand from my mother-in-law, and from my husband, too.

> I want two children, of either sex. I'll have one before 30, another in my early 30s. I plan to work four hours a day for at least 6 to 8 years, while the children are small; I'll be efficient in my work. Parents need to be there with children; they take more care than anyone. My career will not allow me to move to another city. If my husband transfers,

I would stay and ask him to come back soon. I think my husband will respect my issues and wishes.

On another day, I went to her home. Her father said he was not to be quoted due to his highly visible position, so he politely left the room after we had exchanged a few brief remarks. I visited Shruti and her mother and paternal grandmother, who are part of the household. Shruti's mother spoke with me cordially. She married when she was 21; her husband was 26, and had been practicing law for two years. The grandmother shared that she too is a college graduate. There was resistance to her completing college in her day, but she insisted. Shruti says that now females know how to stand up for their rights, and even to stand against their families. For her grandmother to have done so long ago is a source of pride to her.

Shruti's mother contributes her thoughts on plans for Shruti's marriage.

A boy for Shruti should be employed for at least two years; he should be either a doctor, a lawyer, or of another profession, as many years educated as she is, earning well. Shruti will be earning; and if the boy's father is still earning, that income will also be there.

This interest in producing considerable amplitude of income fits well with the economic status of this current family. The lifestyle displayed adds more weight to it.

The household has three cars for the family, one an official car for the judge, and one designated for Shruti to use. The mother is taken by a driver when she needs to go out. She belongs to clubs, ladies' associations, a welfare association, and monthly meetings of judges and their spouses. The ladies talk about fashion, family, and gardening. She loves gardening and has a mali who carries out her designs. She is busy with her children, home, reading, painting, embroidery, knitting, and the stock market. She goes out for shopping or dinner. She and her husband take a walk in a city garden each morning or evening.

Shruti's mother says that her daughter can be out after 8 PM as long as they know she is okay. For internships, though, Shruti is gone for a month at a time, and the family makes no difficulty for her about this. The mother says, "She is becoming mature, and I am also getting mature with her. I've given her good values, and can't spy on her."

Shruti states, "I want to go through a phase where I'm not married, where I'm into my career and am not all that much monitored." Her mother says, "When she's career-wise independent, then things automatically change." Shruti adds: "She's trying to understand my generation, and is becoming more broad-minded than her parents were." Her mother says that her own parents were not comfortable with her having friends home, especially male friends; "They seemed uncomfortable with my birthday party. Now India has more westernization." Shruti explains, "We use that word to mean less orthodox;" and her mother adds, "in terms of male–female relations."

I took a tour of their spacious house. They have five servants, as well as numerous rooms (Ray and Qayum 2009 offer a richly supported definition of the middle class as the servant-employing class). Shruti and her sister share a bedroom with their grandmother. Shruti's own separate room is the one she studies in. There is a well-kept garden. As I was leaving, I passed through the ante-room where Shruti's father's clients waited, after first passing through his study, where he was meeting two of them. Shruti drove me back to my guesthouse in her late-model car.

Shruti is refined, and yet very clear and strong. She is not superficial. Her commitment to her future is powerful and well thought-out. She has all the background to know whereof she speaks. The immense resources of social and cultural capital she possesses in this family lead her to be able to make an ambitious yet manageable career and life plan; she is fully able to translate her background resources and education into real capabilities.[1] It is not surprising that a talented girl of such a successful professional upper-middle-class family should be able to proceed with ease into the new trend of young women having lifetime career plans.

She has spirited back and forth with her mother, who keeps her responses eagerly agreeable. This relationship demonstrates unquestionable warmth of parental support, in which the daughter takes

---

[1]   Hart (2012) links concepts from Bourdieu and Sen in an intriguing way that suggests how this process can work.

the lead and the parent follows. The byplay about orthodoxy is particularly interesting, Shruti wanting to dismiss more of it, her mother only some of it.

What strikes me as unusual is some of her language: "It suits me to be aggressive," pronounced in the same genteel manner as the rest of her self-presentation, but with a sense of moral force. Her hope to follow in her father's footsteps is well supported by his attitudes. He urged me to meet a lady judge whom he offered to introduce, so that I could see one in operation. I note this as his witness to me that what Shruti wants to do and be is quite reasonably possible, and that he fully supports it.

I titled this chapter "Status-raising as a Father–Daughter Project," and I will explore this briefly in relation to Shruti. The family status that I see being enhanced in this father–daughter collaboration seems to me partly to do with espoused professional and ethical ideals. Both the father and the daughter have a stated commitment to help overcome injustice in the position and treatment of women, and to do it through the medium of the law. There is no urgent "need" in the conventional monetary sense for Shruti to pursue a career, any more than for daughters in many other rich families. She is brilliant and able, and seems to follow an inspiration. I think her father is proud of this. When she talked about her aims, her voice was strong; when the topic was marriage, her tone was a bit disparaging. She had a gently nuanced way of guiding her mother to follow along with the process of changing.

This family has no son; but the role of an eldest child, in whom the family is very well pleased, would fall unerringly to this charming and yet firmly determined daughter. No doubt, this kind of family's social status can also be enhanced by having an eminent career woman as one of its products. There is little doubt, either, that this daughter will be able to live very prosperously. She may be able to make considerable money, even during the years that she works part-time from home in order to be near her children. She may be able to almost match the income to be made by her husband (though since the community is Bania, and she would be willing to marry a young businessman, he may in fact become very rich). She could stay at home and be a lady of leisure like her mother; but she urgently wants not to do that. "One thing I'll make sure of—I will continue my work. I'm passionate about it!" she said. She is surely the way she is now with the full approval of her prominent father. The highly assertive style of daughterly behavior that she exhibits is clearly approved of in the upper-middle-class father–daughter project of change represented in this family.

What kind of role model does this newly assertive style of woman provide, and to whom? This behavior, not just confined to the parlors of the wealthy, is also being seen among the newly educated classes whose daughters are moving into new roles. It is being seen, as well, among daughters whose background lacks almost any education, and yet who are now standard bearers for their families. How far can this capability for assertiveness, discovered only individual by individual, serve in redressing the awesome and terrible needs that women in India continue to have? This is not a question this book can answer, but must still, provocatively, pose. Yet returning to where we began, it is clear that fathers play a central role. If we are seeing a shift in gender relations in some families, we are seeing it not only on the part of the daughters but also on the part of the men who are their fathers.

We will continue to consider the part that men play in these stories, and to ask whether the changes they represent in male attitudes may be spreading. And if so, what might be the consequences for the future, not just for women, but for social development more broadly? We will not forget, though, that this is a very selective phenomenon. The sample is representative only of girls whose teachers think highly enough of their career abilities to recommend them to me for this study. How much social change can a set of especially bright and promising young women (and their families) from backgrounds high and low bring about? These questions will be considered in a later chapter.

6

Educated Elites in a New Gender Era

The stories we have read in Chapters 4 and 5 might have given rise to an impression, foreshadowed in Chapter 3, of a teleology of unstoppable social progress as defined by women's empowerment. Aside from other objections to the problematic and often unwarranted expectations of modernization theory, how much actual empowerment is contained in the fact that more young women are now being encouraged to study for lifelong careers? How much subordination, old and new, is hidden in it? Many of the career aspirations, so hopefully held by young women in higher education today, may not be fully borne out in the careers they are able to obtain in the next few years, for reasons that are both economic and sociocultural.

College Education and Women's Employment

India's future economic welfare as the demographic transition continues depends to a considerable extent on the fuller incorporation of women in all realms of social and economic activity. A period of rapid demographic transition is recognized as one in which there can be a demographic dividend, as the bulge in the working-age population, caused by a large youthful population's entering adulthood, allows more rapid economic productivity growth than an age structure more weighted toward older ages. This dividend ends when the transition has completed itself and the age pyramid becomes flatter. The completion of India's transition may take as little as another decade and a half, or be protracted over two or more decades.

For the nation to make use of its working-age surplus in aid of its fuller development, rapid improvements in both education and labor force opportunity for both sexes are required. A lack of gender equality in these inputs will diminish the positive develop-ment effects that could result from the otherwise promising age structure (Edmeades, Malhotra, and Green 2008). It is possible for rapidly growing employment opportunities, if they occur, to become a powerful factor in motivating further rises in the levels of women's educational attainment and qualifications. In the right circumstances, it is also possible for a rapid expansion of higher educational access, which India has been undergoing, to fuel this virtuous cycle. But once the demographic transition is completed, the window of bonus opportunity for speedy economic gains begins to close. A rapid expansion of employment opportunities needs to begin at once, and then be sustained over the remaining years of the demographic transition and on beyond, in order to provide the growth the economy requires.

I first examine the issue of women's employment opportunities, and take up later in the chapter the important question of whether other subordinations still remain in place even for women who succeed in attaining their career goals.

Many of the young women I interviewed are aiming for profes-sions that are, in large part, very specialized, dependent upon niches they are currently already part of and hope to maintain, based on a special set of mentoring relationships they are fortunate enough to be involved in now. Generalized employment data, therefore, will not do justice in registering the validity of the hopes of these particular girls. Nevertheless, we begin by looking at a recent employment table (Table 6.1).

As already seen in Chapter 3, enrollment in higher education in 2010–2011 was 27.5 million, still only about a fifth of the popula-tion aged 18–23. Women are a smaller proportion than men, 44 percent of the total. But Table 6.1 clearly shows us that women who do obtain college degrees have been surging ahead in their *rates* of

Table 6.1

LFPR by education, sex, and residence, age 15+

Year	Education Level	Rural		Urban	
		Male	*Female*	*Male*	*Female*
1999–2000	Literate < Sec	86.4	36.6	82.0	17.9
	Sec + H.Sec	74.7	19.5	68.2	12.7
	Graduate +	89.8	41.0	85.4	30.2
2007–2008	Literate < Sec	86.3	36.3	83.7	17.2
	Sec + H.Sec	72.1	23.5	67.1	11.3
	Graduate +	90.2	49.5	85.7	35.4

Source: Government of India, Ministry of Statistics and Programme Implementation, 2011.

participation in work. Rates are calculated on the basis of the population in a given category. We see an improving rate of employed rural female graduates, though the numbers of those in the basis category (all rural female graduates) are very few, both in relation to graduate males and to graduate urban females. What really stands out in Table 6.1 is that the labor force participation rates of female college graduates, both rural and urban, are growing faster than those of equally educated males. Males are not making significant rate gains, though their work participation rates are still much higher than those of females in both the periods shown. But women are reducing the size of the gap. With 35 percent of urban women with graduate level education and above being employed in 2008, as compared with 30 percent in 2000, this indicates improvement in the fulfillment of career aspirations for many educated women.

We need to ponder the inverse ratios, as well. If 70 percent of urban female graduates in 2000 and 65 percent in 2008 were not employed, how many of these graduates were aspiring career women whose wishes had been denied? (Considering inverse ratios for the male graduates, about 15 percent were not employed in either year. This is an unemployment record of concern; but it is far from the magnitude of women's unemployment.) To get at possible estimates for answers, we could apportion the base populations and age structures of these figures for the two periods, so as to remove both the youngest age group who could not be graduates, and the eldest who would have retired, and then make some estimate about a temporary dropout group in the middle who were caring for their children, but intended to return to full-time work. Others might be assigned to a category (again, only as an estimate) of women staying at home and not planning on having a career.

Before even searching for data to attempt any such estimates, however, we must remember that the real questions being posed here are: What kinds of identities are educated urban women aspiring to? What career ambitions are they fulfilling, and which ones are they giving up? The numerical data we find may not give us any help in answering these questions about women's career aspirations, either fulfilled or denied.

Rustagi (2013) shows that the percentage of urban female workers who are educated is very high in particular employment categories (see Table 6.2). Picking out the most outstanding categories implying professional or semiprofessional use of a college education, this table tells us that 84 percent of all the urban female workers employed in computer-related jobs have higher education, as do 73 percent of those working in finance and 72 percent of those working in education. The far right column indicates that the jobs in these three occupational categories are mostly found within the formal economy.

Table 6.2
Urban female workers in selected activities, 2009–2010

| | *Percent of Workers* | | |
| | *By Education Level* | | |
NIC Codes	*Medium*	*High*	*In Regular Employment*
Financial Intermediation	23	73	80
Computer and Related	10	84	100
Public Administration	36	45	98
Education	23	72	90
Health	51	40	86
Other Service Activities	38	26	29
Total	30	22	44

Source: Rustagi 2013, from NSS Data.

The table tells us nothing about the numbers, however. We saw earlier that women graduates who were absorbed into the workforce in 2005 and 2012 were 5 million and 8 million, respectively (not broken out by residence); so their numbers have grown. But these numbers are still small, and are not actually making an increasing showing in the gender composition of educated employment, because while women graduates (both rural and urban) contributed 8 million women to the workforce in 2012, male employed graduates numbered 36 million. This gives us a 2012 female-to-male educated employment ratio of 22.2 women to every 100 men, a ratio almost the same as that of 2005, when it had been 21.7 to 100.

When we compare these employment findings with educational gains being made by women and girls, the contrast is striking. Let us briefly review the discussion in Chapter 3. By 2011, female literacy, calculated on the basis of the population 7 and over, reached 65.5 percent, a gain of 20.3 percent over 2001, while the male literacy rate of 82.1 percent represented a gain of only 7.4 percent. There were 12 million girls in college. In the four decades since 1971, the number of females studying in higher education had grown by a factor of 17, while males grew by a factor of 6. Young people studying in higher education constituted 17.9 percent of all females and 20.8 percent of all males aged eighteen to twenty-three nationally, proportions coming very close to parity. Young school children by 2011 had reached a level even nearer parity between males and females, presaging an even tighter closing of the gender gap in higher education in the years immediately ahead.

As educated women reach a proportion of the female population so close to that of educated males as a share of the male population, the conundrum of today's urban, educated, career-minded women only increases. Women attending college today may be expecting to have careers in much larger numbers than those who are actually able to realize these hopes. What are the expectations of most college girls today? Are very large numbers of them hoping to become employed in professional roles, and to remain there for most of the years of their adult lives? Or is this a figment of their and their families' imaginations?

Let us examine trends in employment in the organized sector of the Indian economy between 1991 and 2009 (Table 6.3). I have divided an 18-year-long annual employment series into two nine-year blocks for comparability, and we will see that there is an important difference between the two periods. Organized sector jobs are regular, formal jobs, not only those being done by educated people. Jobs in the organized sector are not limited to cities, though they are nevertheless mostly located in urban locations. This table therefore does not show populations broken out by either level of education or urban residence. But the organized employment sector still, in fact, contains the lion's share of the educated urban employed population.

Table 6.3
Employment in the organized sector, India

Year, Ending 31 March	Total in Millions	Proportion Female	No. Women in Millions	Proportion Male	No. Men in Millions
1991	26.730	0.141	3.769	0.859	22.961
2000	27.960	0.176	4.921	0.824	23.039
Change, 1991–1999	4.6%	24.8%	30.6%	–4.1%	0.3%
2009	28.098	0.199	5.592	0.801	22.506
Change, 2000–2009	0.5%	13.1%	13.6%	–2.8%	–2.3%

Source: Government of India, Ministry of Statistics and Programme Implementation, 2011: Table 7, 56.

Reviewing this table, in 2009, there were 28 million people employed in the organized sector. Almost 20 percent of those, or about 5.6 million, were women. Over the two periods, women have been gaining a share of the organized sector which men are losing. These gains were particularly fast in the nine years from 1991 to 2000, when women increased both their numbers and their proportions impressively, while men stagnated in both. In the second period demarcated here, women increased by a smaller proportion relative to what they gained in the earlier period; but men actually became both a lesser proportion and a lower number. The beginning of the 21st century did not display as much of a "boom" in organized employment, including both professional and semiprofessional employment, as the end of the 20th century did. In regard to women, it was just a small leap forward in relation to the potential.

Referring to state tables, after considering the number and relative size of the cities in each state, I have roughly estimated that as recently as 2009, women working in organized sector jobs may have been fewer than 100,000 in Vadodara, fewer than 400,000 in Bengaluru, fewer than 500,000 in Mumbai, and fewer than 100,000 in Allahabad.

The financial crisis that began at the end of 2008 does not show a large effect in the employment series shown in Table 6.3; effects stemming from it can be found in more recent data. The high-tech sector, particularly the IT-enabled services portion of it that includes BPO), has been particularly affected due to its extreme international vulnerability. Before the financial crisis that has recently beset the US and Europe, the foreign demand for labor outsourced to India had been growing, spreading into urban areas where it had not existed before. There were inflated hopes about a massive growth in this sector, one which is responsible for a large share of India's international trade revenue.

Its development added new well-paid jobs for women to the labor market. But its relative magnitude, in terms of the numbers of jobs needed by educated women, remained extremely small. Employment in BPO facilities serving international clients reached a national total of 409,000 in 2006, climbing to 704,000 in 2008. The industry had high hopes that this rate of growth would continue or be surpassed. By 2010, however, growth had slowed greatly; there were just 770,000 jobs in that year (Taylor, D'Cruz, Noronha and Scholarios 2014: 107). Women were approximately 30 percent of these employees; they had about 123,000 BPO jobs in 2006 and about 231,000 in 2010.

This slice of the employment pool of college-educated women remains nearly insignificant in size. Of an estimated three million urban educated women employed in 2010 nationally, the number given above would be less than 8 percent. What proportion would that number be of all the urban educated women who might be qualified for this type of job? Those would be women educated up to 12th standard or above, proficient and fluent in English. That is clearly a moot question. Although girls with 12th standard educations may be included in the tiny total, most of these jobs have been claimed by college graduates. These jobs, though well-paid, are unstable, difficult to hold on to, hard on people's health, and often not a fit match for a college degree, in addition to being very few. Yet they remain desirable, both for the money and for other reasons.

Reflections from Bengaluru

A number of young women who had held such jobs for a time were interview subjects during my 2005 research in Bengaluru. I turn to that experience now to discuss some of the motivations and aspirations of such English-speaking college-educated women, and the commitment many of them felt to become professionals, someday, somehow.

I begin with two sisters who had professional degrees, and had worked in call centers for a while to help support their parents when their father was severely injured. Seema had an architecture degree, and her older sister Revathi had a law degree. When we met, neither was employed either in a call center or in the professional field in which she had a qualification. Seema had quit in dissatisfaction and Revathi had left because she was in a late stage of pregnancy. Seema was contemptuous of the experience she had had at her call center, while Revathi, by contrast, had been pursuing promotions in hers. Seema said, "If you are really career-oriented, you will not work in a call center; it spoils your real career." This was her expression of disgust and disappointment about how things were turning out for her. She was only taking tuitions at the time; this was nowhere near an architecture career. She wanted just to quit and get married and be supported, because she was fed up.

Revathi was mentioned in Chapter 5 as expressing herself with assertiveness. She was married and expecting a child. With enthusiastic support from her husband, she also planned to have a lifelong career.

> I am doing a Masters in Business Law by correspondence, with class-es on weekends. Being the legal advisor to a firm is my real career. Unless you get really good growth in the call center industry, it is a

monotonous job. But you get a lot to learn, such as communication skills and proficiency in English.

She intended to garner all the good she could out of this experience, gaining more of what she saw as professional qualities. Some of her motivation lay in the changes she had brought to her natal family, helping support them when there was a need, gaining respect for herself, and seeing her mother begin to go out of the house and enjoy doing things she had never done before. "Let me be an example," she said. She hoped to be an example for other women, and to help keep alive the hopes of women seeking to become professionals. She did not know if she would rejoin the call center workforce, or succeed in finding a law job later on. But she felt transformed by the two years' work in the call center and by all that it had afforded to her family, from one kind of woman to another.

Call centers, set up to serve customers abroad over the telephone, and employing only a tiny sliver of the population, require good English. College-educated people are overqualified for the work, but they have the needed facility in the language and have been able to get there first to grasp the early opportunities. What is needed is usually convent-school style English, which implies a certain level of eliteness within this population.

These young college-educated women in Bengaluru who had worked in call centers and other high-tech service jobs, had very definite ideas about what these job opportunities and experiences had meant to them, and about how these experiences had changed their perceptions about their own futures. In essence, it seemed to them that new ideas about possible forms of gender relations were emerging in response to these new job opportunities. Certain trends emerged. Almost all of the women in the study intended to use or had already successfully used the BPO job as a stepping-stone on the way to a more promising career. Some had used the money to pay for further education, training, or qualifications. This was possible due to the support of most of their families, those who did not require them to contribute most of their income, but rather encouraged them to save it for themselves and their own advancement. There was a level of eliteness in this factor, too.

Most of the study group wanted to have an arranged marriage; only a few preferred to select their own partner. The youngest women (20–22) expected their marriages to be arranged by about the age 24. Those a year or two older thought they might be able to wait until 26. Women under 24 said they would move to where the groom would be located for his career, but that they planned to continue to participate in the labor force, however they could manage to do so. Women over 24, by contrast, said that husband and wife should bargain about where they would live or where they would move, in order to further one or both careers.

Each woman insisted she intended to pursue a career throughout her life. Most said that they might take off work for about two years at the birth of each child. The number of children desired varied between two and zero. Employment problems in India did not cast any shadow over the sunny optimism of these young women, who believed that they would ultimately succeed in having good careers throughout their lives. Each woman had demands regarding the husbands they would accept. While they wanted their parents to perform most aspects of the traditional role in arranging the marriage, they had told their parents that they wanted a husband who would support them in having a full career throughout their lives. They wanted to have an arranged, or semi-arranged, marriage, with very compatible in-laws, in order to ensure a harmonious family support system for themselves and their children.

There was a sense of opportunity, but behind it, there was a strong sense of pressure. The young people I talked to were fortunate: they had needed work, and they had work. Several of them required the jobs they had obtained because without them they could not fulfill both their own goals and those of their families. None of them was primarily working to support parents, although helping parents was part of each story, especially for two whose mothers were widowed. The greater need that they and their middle-class parents had was for them to move ahead into a life of career security.

The 2007 paper analyzed changes in the rationale and methods of "arranging" a marriage, proposing that steady income might be seen as a substitute for dowry. Income-earning capacity may become a dowry in its own right. These women did not believe that their parents would need to provide a dowry for their marriages. Their confident stance about this was a thin veil, protecting them from frankly recognizing that their parents could not provide the kind of dowry that would marry them well.

This casts light on choices the parents had made two and three decades ago. This valuing of daughters, seeking the best education and opportunities for them, had been practiced by families who were neither very rich nor very highly educated at least two decades before the liberalization of the Indian economy. It could be seen as having been a lucky gamble, this betting on girls. The young women I met in that project were from families where education for both sexes had long been held in high value, although many of the parents, both fathers and mothers, had not reached the level of college graduation themselves.

Education and the Professions

Regarding the same time period which the earlier Bengaluru research comes from, the following data (Table 6.4) are available for all the four states being examined in the current research, as well as for all India (from Sahni and Shankar 2012).

Table 6.4
Total numbers of girl students in higher education

	1958–1959	*% of National*	*2004–2005*	*% of National*
Gujarat	5,249	3.58	274,198	5.90
Karnataka	7,236	4.93	313,202	6.74
Maharashtra	22,362	15.25	577,892	12.40
Uttar Pradesh	12,237	8.34	581,460	12.58
India	146,575	100.00	4,641,576	100.00

Source: Sahni and Shankar 2012: 243.

What this table shows is both the truly vast expansion of higher education since Independence, and the remarkable growth of its availability to women. The more than four and a half million women in college in 2005 were 32 times as many as there had been in 1959. Gujarat, Karnataka, and Uttar Pradesh had progressively increased their share of the nation's girl students. Maharashtra was a leading provider of female education early, and continued to be a very large one. These four states together provided higher education to 38 percent of the nation's female college students in 2005.

Sahni and Shankar's article takes it as a point of concern, however, that "boys remain better represented across various disciplines" (2012: 242), while "girls are confined/concentrated in selective disciplines" (2012: 244). This concern coincides with their definition of "professional education" as being represented by engineering and medicine, subjects that are rapidly being taken up by private educational institutions charging heavy fees. Arts and commerce, in which the nation's college girls tend to be concentrated, they define in contrast as "general education." This is an unnecessarily narrow vision of professionalism, as it appears within the occupational diversity found in India today.

The Oxford Online Dictionary, as its first definition of a "professional" (as a noun), gives us "a person engaged or qualified in a profession." The same source then calls a profession "a paid occupation, especially one that involves prolonged training and a formal qualification." An older collegiate dictionary, however (Webster's New World Dictionary, 1960), calls a profession "a vocation or occupation requiring advanced training in some liberal art or science, and usually involving mental rather than manual work, as teaching, engineering, writing, etc.; especially medicine, law, or theology (formerly called *the learned professions*)." It is very worthwhile to remember these much older roots of this idea, which have echoes in the cultural capital we observe in the self-presentation of some of the interview subjects.

For now, however, we must define "professionalism." Its first definition, according to the Oxford Online Dictionary, used here once again because of its being contemporary, is "the competence or skill expected of a professional." A definition this online dictionary gives of "professional" as an adjective is that it means "participating for gain or livelihood in an activity or field of endeavor often engaged in by amateurs." The performance of activities that many engage in for recreation is commodified by others in order to provide entertainment for pay. But more relevant to our discussion, another definition of "professional" (as an adjective) given by Merriam-Webster Online, is the following: "requiring specialized knowledge and often long and intensive academic preparation."

In terms of what makes for professionalism via educational attainment, two young women whom I met at Allahabad University, Tamara and Tanika, stand out. Both of them have strongly assertive attitudes, coupled with the polished behavior and manner of address which a few of my other research subjects share. They also appear to display a mastery of the knowledge and skills required to be able to become professionals in recognizable ways. These attributes, it becomes clear, are linked with the fact that both are Brahmins, with the culture of the value of education extending back several generations. Shruti, also upper-caste, has the same assurance and eliteness. Tamara and Tanika are additionally impressive for their fluently incorporated, passionately expressive uses of knowledge gained through their college educations in talking about their beliefs and missions in life. Tanika is planning to be a philosophy professor, and Tamara intends to become an international lawyer. Though both were attending Allahabad University when I met them, they did not know each other, studied in separate faculties, and had separate personal styles and separate kinds of families.

Tanika is 23, has her B.A. and M.A. and is now pursuing her D.Phil., all in philosophy. She has one sibling, a younger brother who is in college. Her father has a B.A. and a technical diploma. Having been an engineer, he now works for an insurance company. The mother is a housewife with an M.A.; we have met her earlier, in Chapter 2. The family is not wealthy. Their house is old, partitioned, and re-formed for two sets of families, with very small old rooms with dark ceiling beams and door frames. In the center is a courtyard and staircase to an upstairs floor where the uncles and their families stay. Tanika has lived here with her joint family always.

Like Vimla, she has a junior research fellowship from the University Grants Commission (UGC), and has been selected as a lecturer. The fellowship pays ₹19,200 a month, plus travel and contingencies for three years. If there is a vacancy and she passes an interview, a senior research fellowship can be awarded, paying up to ₹31,000 per month. "I may be done in two or three years, and may be settled in a job then, or even before. When my 6-month pre-doctoral program certificate is done, I will apply for jobs. Having the certificate is mandated by the UGC before applying." Thus, she may finish her D.Phil. and not even require the SRF if she obtains a regular job.

Tanika tells me she wants to have influence for the betterment of society. An academic career teaching philosophy, for which she has obtained top marks, won prizes, and compiled some experience, would allow her to influence many people. She says that Allahabad University and Delhi University have the best philosophy departments in the country. She explains,

> For my marriage, I am not eager to meet anyone too soon. My parents want a well-settled man from a good family, of the same caste, religion, earning and financial independence level. For my sake, he should be independent, a good person, and respect me and my feelings. My career is progressing; he should not ask me to leave it. The freedom of women in India is still conditional.

Parents give daughters *some* freedoms, but her husband should allow her all the freedom that she wants. "My parents allow me to take decisions; I want a husband like this, too, and more! He should ask my opinions, have dialogue, and we should take most of our decisions together. I should be free to take decisions regarding my career."

Tanika follows these remarks with a rhetorical statement of the positions she holds on the status of women.

> Women are realizing they also ought to participate economically. We are made for production and not just reproduction. Sustainable development can't occur only with males; the country will develop only if women too are in the labor force. There's a shift of ideology and revolutionized ideals. We are not just puppets in their hands. It's not just about money, but about individual visibility. We are currently the invisible ones. Men and women should be equal. The emphasis has to be on education.

Visiting her home later, I ask her parents why they support a career for a daughter. Her father answers that both literacy and awareness have increased. "After marriage, without education there are many problems: if there is a tragedy, the mother is not able to work, teach the children properly, or go outside alone. Confidence and self-dependence are necessary now. Older people didn't allow it due to security reasons." The mother said that she does not go out alone (see Chapter 2). "We want our daughter to go out and go farther," her mother says.

Tanika's father says,

> We want her to earn her livelihood. There used to be one earning member in a family, but now both are needed to prevent loss due to accident or disability. The grandparents are very supportive, and wanted their girls to study even in their time, but then it was not so possible. Allahabad was always modern, but now it is even more modern still. Literature, education and culture were the main domains, but now there are more modern subjects as well.

> Let her first achieve her target, and then we'll talk about her marriage. The same caste would be our first preference. There will be no dowry to be given—just some gifts for the home. The groom should have the same level of education as she does, and be employed or in government service in Class 1.

This is a family that is not wealthy. They have valued education for several generations, but many of the members have not attained much of it. The father is less educated than the mother, due to family issues that detained him in his youth, but she does not work, and he is the support of his part of the family. He has expressed the need for his wife to be equipped to step in and take over his franchise if his health fails. His brothers and their families live in the same rather cramped building.

Tanika's younger brother is studying for his B.Tech. degree. Tanika is not going to be needed to support her parents in their old age; from their point of view, she is being educated so she can be a support to her marital family in the future. From her point of view, though, the purpose of her education is to support and illuminate her interests and values, while providing her with a career that she believes in. One of her strongly held values is that women should live productive lives. With that in view, she has been at the top of her class, given impressive public presentations, and won prizes.

Tanika's personal style is modest and unassuming. She is a kind person. Her excellence is understated; she carries herself with a gentle but unself-conscious pride. She reminds me of other educated people of high caste, living in rather humble circumstances, whom I knew in earlier decades. Some of the young people had a brilliance that carried them into fascinating careers. Among various families of my acquaintance in decades past, those were the boys. Now this type of family is producing girls who can attain not only degrees, but also careers. These families carried then, and still carry now, the marks of gentility. This is the cultural capital they carry forward. Tanika's parents possess a memory image of an Allahabad of long ago, filled with culture, literature, and old-world elegance; and now they are willing to embrace a new image of the city, fit for today. In this new image, it would be perfectly suitable, and indeed very pleasing, to have a highly educated, professionally successful daughter.

Tamara is a different kind of young woman than others I met on this project. She reminds me more of students I have met in recent years at the Jawaharlal Nehru University (JNU) or the Indian Institutes of Technologies (IITs), or of Indian students at Berkeley and Stanford in the US. She seemed supremely confident in her role as one of the leaders of a student group at the Allahabad Law Faculty, which does outreach to provide legal aid to people in need. She speaks in the style of a long-standing urbanite, and looks and dresses like one, as well.

She has lived in different cities with her family and attended convent schools in each. Her father, who has a Ph.D., is a professor at the university. Previously he taught at other colleges in other cities. His wife is college educated and stays at home. Tamara has a younger sister and a younger brother. When I visited her home, they all joined in to entertain me, conversing in a lively manner. They wanted to ask me many questions, and we even debated various topics. They talked about how much they all enjoy one another's company, taking trips as a family together. The apartment was very modern, but not large. Tamara had driven to pick me up and take me to her home in the family car.

Tamara was 22 when I met her, and in her fifth year of the law program at the Allahabad University, a five year integrated course, granting degrees of B.A. and L.L.B. Honors. She said that the entrance exam was challenging, including current affairs, a general knowledge of history, international issues, English and math. Tamara has shown flying colors in her studies all along.

> Oh, yes, I do plan to work throughout my life. I want to be independent. I am a staunch feminist. I study gender law now, and I'd like to specialize in it as much as possible. There are special legislations for women, such as the Domestic Violence Act and the Sexual Harassment Act. Since India is a signatory to the UN's CEDAW, international norms are also relevant. Rape is covered by national law under the Indian Penal Code. There are several national commissions working for the upliftment of women.

> After finishing this year, I'll take a Master's degree, a one-year LLM program, probably abroad. My family is open to sending me abroad for further studies. My mother always says that a woman should be independent. She knows I've been ambitious since early years. I have done public speaking. Surrounded by lawyers, I've been impressed with this as a career.

> For the past decade, we've been upper-middle-class. All three children have studied in private schools. My sister is in 11th standard and wants to be a doctor. Marriage plans don't exist for me right now. My parents say by 26 or so, I ought to get married; I say 27 or 28, if I do get married.

She has dated, and they know and are comfortable with this. She is seeing someone in Delhi when she is there on law internships. But more than wanting to focus on that relationship, she says, "I want to study! I may start my own law firm, doing either civil or criminal, some pro bono, plus human rights. I want to apply it here." She says only maybe to marriage, but adds that her mother says, "Single people are not appreciated in India. Be a professional, but end up with a family. You need company in life." She adds, "I will trust my parents' judgment in introducing me to a boy. I say absolutely No to dowry—There's a law against it! It's helpful to marry someone in the same profession; you can understand each other's issues."

> I would not want a joint family; I've never lived in one. I'll have servants to look after the kids, no more than two. It's important to spend time with children. But there should be no limits on my ambition. Both husband and wife should make decisions about expenses. My husband's parents should be like my boyfriend's, who are cool with professional women. With money in my own account, I want to donate some and invest in good works.

She carries very little cash now. "I tell my parents what I need: car costs, lunch, and so on. Later on, I will use my own earnings to further my goals."

I noticed that Tamara was more dominant on campus than she was at home. On campus, she had a very assertive style that was also uniquely sophisticated, as shown by the tone in the interview material quoted above. Other examples of assertiveness have been looked at closely in Chapter 5, but none of those others were so almost breezy about it, so filled with an implicit authority glossing the fervent idealism. Most others also did not pack their answers to my career questions with so much relevant, educated knowledge.

At home, Tamara went along with the family's jolly togetherness, dominated by her lively father, who wanted to provide opinions on all topics. Later I saw her again briefly, and she hinted that she had not agreed with some of the opinions he expressed. He had given me a rationale for why marriage within one's caste is very important. This may have been one of the areas where she had politely disagreed, but without saying so.

Intending to do her Masters, Tamara has succeeded in getting a placement abroad. Unless she is dissuaded, which I believe she will not allow, it seems she will continue exploring opportunities abroad so as to fulfill her ambition for an international law career.

Shruti, Tanika, and Tamara represent educated elites in a new gender era, in which women's full careers are newly embraced by their natal families. There seems a rather strong likelihood in their cases that this embrace of their careers will prevail in their marital families, as well. The pool of eligible matches who have very much the same ideas about career women is almost certainly more plentiful in their social circles than it is in the cases of Vasanti in Mumbai, or Priya in Vadodara.

The acceptance of a daughter's career ambitions, among castes already long since middle class, is spreading to smaller and more conservative cities than before, and into families who formerly did not approve of such plans. Yet even as it seems highly likely that these three upper-caste girls will, upon successfully obtaining employment, succeed in sustaining their careers after marrying, it is obvious that none of them has rejected outright the conventions underlying arranged marriage within caste. All three of them can be seen as feminist without being more broadly socially progressive, or holding an ideology in which feminism is embedded in a wider social critique. "We are not just puppets in their hands," as Tanika puts it; this is a brave and ringing credo, and yet this feminist stance can be seen as being privatized, even privileged, if it remains focused on one-to-one relationships within couples and families. Tanika wants to have good influence in society more widely, by becoming a philosophy professor in a great public university; yet she does not seem thus far to challenge within-caste marriage as a social structural bulwark of inequality.

It is striking to witness the complacency about the convention of within-caste arranged marriage in the case of the two law students, Tamara and Shruti, whose families are well-to-do and whose own careers promise to be rather lucrative. From a financial point of view, they will likely have opportunity to support themselves adequately, and will probably have the freedom to discover desirable partners on their own. Both Shruti and Tamara, in an unusual claim, also said that they wanted to live separately from their parents for a time. In her memorable statement, made right in front of her mother, Shruti had said, "I want to go through a phase where I'm not married, where I'm into my career and am not all that much monitored."

These women's moves toward greater independence as career women, however, will probably not stop their parents from pressuring them about making a match and setting a date to get married. If either of them has not selected her own partner by the time the pressure becomes intense, she may find it convenient simply to comply.

Sophisticated Tamara, who had a boyfriend yet was not serious, due to her plan to continue her studies abroad, said, "I will trust my parents' judgment in introducing me to a boy." She hinted to me later that she does not always agree with her professor father. If she does not become engaged to her friend, perhaps she might gracefully accept a match within her caste after an introduction arranged by her parents, without asking any questions as to whether within-caste marriage is actually in line with a logically coherent and socially critical feminist position.

The intersectionality of gender, caste, and arranged marriage is deeply systemic, in ways that not all women's studies or other gender-sensitivity courses, which many of my research subjects were exposed to, may have fully encompassed in their curricula. No one has been more articulate about this than Uma Chakravarti (2003). "Caste cannot be reproduced without endogamy …[which is] a tool for the perpetuation of caste and gender subordination," she writes (2003: 27). She argues further, "Because the status of the entire extended family is contingent upon a proper marriage, it is deemed to be too important a decision to leave to the persons actually getting married" (2003: 33).

This does not currently imply that upper-middle-class parents allow no leeway at all. And even if their approval of a proposed marriage is based mainly upon their concern for their own status within their most crucial extended family networks, in some cases those networks may now have widened beyond the family's immediate caste to include others that (in a new context) have gained equal hierarchical stature. Yet social status and rank remain inviolate considerations.

I now return to the question of whether other subordinations still remain in place for women, even those who do attain their career goals. Workplace issues for women's lives, which are both interesting and important, have found little place in this book, since we are mainly concerned with women before work. But the kinds of private subordination that will impact young working women—however professional their jobs are—will be found within their homes, and in the families they belong to on both natal and marital sides. Most of these young women, as they expressed themselves in the interviews, will likely remain subordinate and agreeable to the requirement to manage their marital households. Equality in homecare responsibilities of husband and wife may be the ideal, but it is doubtful if it will be fully met. The most highly placed professional women will be able to have full-time help from servants in several capacities. The managing of them will be primarily the woman's job.

The management of money will be another issue for negotiation within their marital homes. Singh and Bhandari (2012), in an article on money management in joint families, write, "The ideology of the partnership of marriage does not focus solely on the togetherness of the couple, but is placed within the context of a harmonious extended family" (2012: 46).This is a matter about which each of my interview subjects seemed to have firm intentions. They wish to help support themselves and their most important others, which may include their own parents as well as their husbands, children, and in-laws.

With regard to the care of children, most of the subjects imagine combining this task with others, sometimes multiple others. The most desirable option about child rearing, to almost all of them throughout the four cities, is to have an older woman in the home who is an actual member of the family. This includes, for example, the case of Sonam from Nagpur, whose orphaned fiancé's aunt is planning to live with them, to Sonam's great delight. A young wife may arrive at a higher or lower level in the household pecking order than some of these live-in relatives, but there will be a great deal of relationship work for them to do. Negotiations may favor the young wife or they may not.

Sometimes my interviewees even envision their own mothers coming to help them, quite unlike the strict customs of separation and reserve that have constrained parents of married daughters in past generations among the upper castes. Tanika's parents, for example, both said they would like to go to her home and help with her children. The glue of love will help soothe difficulties. But it may not provide a woman with all the freedom she hopes for in her career life.

It was striking to hear Tamara's supreme confidence in saying, "I'll have servants to look after the kids … It's important to spend time with children. But there should be no limits on my ambition." The idea of no career limits for a married working woman with children is a tall order in many societies today. Some possible limits may even derive from feelings a woman might experience after children arrive, and the combination of roles she then might find herself wanting to play.[1] The alleviation of limits will depend on the sincere and thoroughgoing support of others. These others (aging parents, perhaps) then will have legitimate claims of their own, which may present limits of some kinds. Any such conflicts and crosscurrents that might lie ahead, however, were not yet visible to Tamara. What her own actual wishes regarding childcare might be in her life ahead were not yet fully accessible for her to consider and plan for.

Educated elites in this new gender era will surely maintain much of the underlying and ongoing social order, even as these privileged young women grow into professional roles and identities that are of benefit to them, their families, and those they serve. Their behaviors which continue the maintenance of the social order, however, may prove to be softer and more porous than those of their older relatives. They will have much to consider, perhaps, about the need for a greater congruence between their own educated idealism and the improvement of the status of people in subordinate positions who work for them.

They may even come to reflect on the very nature of the system of sociocultural dominance in which they are so intricately involved. According to Ganguly-Scrase and Scrase (2008),

> Entering the world of work has allowed [women] to gain self-confidence, respect and autonomy. Yet, while some opportunities have arisen to challenge pre-existing gender ideologies, … ultimately

---

[1] A point of reference showing cross-cultural similarity in regard to these statements is found in Damaske (2011), *For the Family? How Class and Gender Shape Women's Work*. Based on recent research in New York, it concludes that women across the board tend to rationalize working as a way to help their families, and to shy away from claiming their actual desire to fulfill their own potential and enjoy their careers in and for themselves.

[women's] challenges are contained within the confines of the patriarchal ideologies of the neoliberal state. (2008: 104).

Some of these women may rise to meet these challenges and begin
to think them through. Even just thinking about them will begin to
make a difference in how they conduct the rest of their lives.

7

Embedded Agency: Gains, Losses, and Unborn Hopes

The young women we have been following often seem valiant and inspiring. They are gaining a self-identity of respect both in the outside world and within their families, which makes their lives ahead very exciting to look forward to. We cannot fail to notice that most of these young women are supported in important ways by multiple others. They receive moral support from their parents, most particularly from their fathers. Many have been aided by public policies in effect during the last two decades. Most are also currently benefitting from the spread of globalized neoliberalism, a sword that divides as well as conquering.

Globalized neoliberalism, with its economic growth potential focused in cities, may bring significant gains for some of those newly entering the middle class; some of those who are enhancing already long-held positions there; and others, less socially advantaged and poor, who are able to gain education, skills, and job market luck. But the current trend may also bring losses which cripple the hopes of many others in the current generation. Though some families and family groups will move up in socioeconomic status, reaching an improved level which they are keen to maintain, the lack of a more robust, broadly-based process of growth in employment than neoliberalism can possibly bring about will thwart the ambitions of other young people and their families. The current retrenchment of funding for large social provisioning schemes will harm others. And a lack of social and economic development in the rural sector will continue to escalate pressures for greater urbanization, a trend which itself may occur without adequate levels of infrastructure development of all kinds.

In this chapter, we look at various kinds of gains and losses to be found among the stories of young women in this study. Several of the stories hold themes of precious gain; we also ask whether they also display corresponding losses, or signify some drawbacks in the new way of life these young women are seeking. We examine arenas of self-definition not even considered by most of these young women, which occur more frequently to girls whose mothers have had careers of their own. We then consider the noncareer mothers of this study and their trajectory through time, and reflect on how their situations add to our understanding of gender relations. Finally, we return to the young women in our sample and examine their deep embeddedness in their families, in connection with the neoliberal trend and its implications for the future.

Gains and Losses

The greatest gain among all my interviews was the story of *Neela*, in Vadodara, who had gained her very life—a life that she might not even have had the chance to have. A sex-selective abortion was being considered when her mother was pregnant with her. But that plan was not ultimately carried out. What resulted was a family happy to have two promising daughters, not at all regretting the lack of a son.

Neela's mother, after having a girl the first time, had been urged by her mother-in-law not to have another daughter. When she became pregnant for the second time, she learned via ultrasound that she would have another girl, and planned to abort due to her mother-in-law's wishes. She told me this herself during my visit to her home. "But my husband said to me, 'We will not tell her that we are having another daughter.' So I cancelled the appointment." When the couple saw their new baby, they were thrilled, and went and showed her with pride to the mother-in-law. "Did you see how good looking she is?" Neela's mother asked me. "She was beautiful, even as a newborn baby."

I met Neela in the Faculty of Family and Community Sciences at the Maharaja Sayajirao University. Born in 1992 into the Patel community, she is tall and willowy with green eyes. She was in her final year for the B.Sc. in fashion design. "I thought of being an air hostess," she said, "but society believes that air hostesses are just sophisticated waitresses." She excels in creative activities like design and dance, and has also done some modeling. Fashion design is a good fit for her.

Neela's father has a B.Com. degree, and works as a bank manager. Her mother's education in Hyderabad was interrupted before she could complete a degree. Neela said,

> My mother did some college and then dropped out when her marriage took place.

> Her father was teaching in Hyderabad, but the family is from Gujarat, and has connections throughout this region. We have a five-village community to choose from here. My father's family is from one village, and my mother's is from another.

> My elder sister is 26 and living at home. She's a dentist, and completed her studies at Mangalore, with a five year course from the best school in her field. She'll soon have her marriage arranged. I'll be married after about five or six years. I would prefer a love marriage, but if my parents introduce someone, I want to have plenty of time to get to know him. My sister has the same requirement. She was asked to meet someone, but the time was too short before a decision was required, and she said no. It's a lifetime decision! Wrong decisions sometimes show fraud. Our parents say, 'If you have a boyfriend, it will be fine, as long as he is a Gujarati Hindu.' My sister wants to study further outside of India; she's a career-oriented girl. If she doesn't marry first, she can go alone. But she hopes to marry and then go abroad. Our parents will see to it that the guy is educated and making a living.

> I don't have a boyfriend now, but I want a boyfriend to become my husband. I have a friendship circle with boys in it. Sometimes my guy friends are many! I'm a dancer, and the dance classes have guys in

them. I teach dancing in the dance academy where I studied. I was one of India's top 30 couple dancers on a TV show! I'm passionate about it, but I've left it now for my studies.

I was not good in theoretical things, and did not get high marks. But now my teachers are proud of me. I won third place last year in a fashion design competition, along with a partner, and we got a job contract for one year—a paid internship in Surat with a good sari brand. I and my design partner negotiated to join after graduation. We will live in Surat in a relative's house, or in our own place. The job will pay 15 thousand per month salary. This can increase if you choose to stay and get a permanent position.

I am career-oriented, and my parents prefer this, rather than having me sitting at home. They want me to support myself. I had a one-month internship in Mumbai and stayed alone there. My dad was supportive in every way. But if I'd been asked out for a holiday with friends, he'd have said no. If a trip was related to education and career, he would allow. My parents know their girls are sensible enough to stay inside limits. Friends might not behave well, but we would judge. Mom came to drop me in Mumbai—she saw it was a safe place, and all okay.

I haven't thought about having kids yet; but both parents should care for them. I would love to live in a joint family. I'll make sure my husband knows that working is something I'm not going to stop, and that he can convey this to his parents. Parents-in-law today don't mind women working. The ladies of my mom's age will not be working, but today's generation is more career-oriented. Women between my age and my mom's age are now working. Change is coming fast. But we can still handle our houses very well! I will give my parents some of my money; they have no son.

When I went to visit Neela's family home in Vadodara, her mother, speaking excellent English, was friendly and outgoing toward me, with Neela leaving us mostly to ourselves. Most of my interview at Neela's home, in fact, was with her mother.

Neela's mother grew up in Hyderabad and was home-schooled until age seven, when a friend of her father's advised him that she would need school qualifications for social purposes. Her father was a professor.

She was a bright girl, entering school at a higher level than her age, and finishing earlier, too. "I wanted to go to medical school. My father put his arm around me and told me that I would become too qualified for the boys they could hope to find back in Gujarat." Her brother found her a well-qualified, successful man in their marriage circle. "We were always happy with what our parents did. My brother saw the boy and said to me, 'This is the one.' My husband-to-be was working as an officer in the State Bank of India, and had already built his house. I moved here." She and I were sitting together in the very same house.

"Now, people coming from this background are well educated," she said.

> There are five brothers and one sister in my husband's family. They all have their own houses and jobs in Baroda, except the one who's in Anand. Some members of the family are now abroad. My father-in-law had died when my husband was in 4th standard in the village. The elder brother had a job in Baroda, so the rest of the family moved here and stayed together. The village was too far away from education. My husband started working with the bank right after 10th standard. In 1981 he bought land and built this house, and in 1986 we got married.

When they married, he was 33. His wife is 10 years younger. He had started bank work early, and later he took a break and went to college for his Bachelors' degree.

> From the beginning, what I did not get, I wanted my children to get. Neela says that I understand the era we are living in now very well! This is not an orthodox family; my daughters are not brought up that way. Neela is going out for basketball; I too played it in school.

Neela now appeared at the door after changing into sports gear and said goodbye to me, and my interview with her mother continued.

> My husband told me that child molding is important. 'Don't get them molded by servants,' he said. 'Give good qualities to your daughters.' I did wish to work, and wanted my mother-in-law to live here with me to help. But she was living with my sister-in-law, looking after her kids. I have made sure my daughters have a good education. I visited their classes and their teachers, in order to keep in touch with this.

Neela and her sister went to a government English-medium school in Baroda. One teacher said to me, 'Are you really a Patel? Patel women are not educated.'[1] But I have been able to train and tutor my daughters, and have never needed outside tuitions for them! I am satisfied with whatever they are becoming.

Neela's parents have been seeing men for their elder daughter, Neela's older sister. Some whom they have met "were not a proper match," the mother said. "Any Gujarati guy will be fine as a match; but the couple should understand each other. Profession will be their priority. I want a very well-educated guy, from a very good family who are not necessarily so educated but are capable of understanding their daughter-in-law. Everyone now sees that education and profession are priorities." Although this last statement contradicts her actual experience of meeting families with less professionally oriented sons, her generalization suggests an optimistic sense on her part that people of her community, as well as others who would be acceptable to them, are rising in education level nowadays.

I met Neela's sister and her father briefly; they had a certain refined quality. Their mid-sized house is comfortably arranged with modern furniture, conveniences, and decor. Neela's mother walked me to the corner to get a taxi, urging me to visit them again. It was a remarkable visit. The decision against female foeticide on the part of the father struck me as ground-breaking. Learning about it turned a corner in research of mine, which had formerly concerned itself with sex selection among members of this same community (Clark 1983). That practice continues, but this family (among others) has become an exception.

Neela's mother, the daughter of a professor who provided personal home-schooling to his own children during their early years, has herself been deeply involved with the education of her children, and has helped produce two independent-minded young women. She poured herself into this with all her talents. She expressed no suppressed bitterness about being kept from her desire to go to medical school and have a career; instead, she described her father affectionately putting his arm around her to explain why this could

---

[1]   See Note 2.

not be. "We were always happy with what our parents did," she said. Her avowed contentment did not refer to the fulfillment of any of the claims she might have wanted to make, but rather, it depended upon educated decisions made by the men in her life. Her husband setting a bar on what his mother could dictate regarding the survival of his daughter was an outstanding instance.

There is tremendous gain in Neela's story; the concomitant losses for her appear very few. Her mother's story, it is true, contains disappointments, but these have been transformed into hopes. But some things may be marked at least as shadows. This family has fairly lost its village roots. The father's family members, after leaving the village, used to live together in the city and support one another; later they all split up to live in separate houses and pursue separate lives. Education and professionalism became the priority in this small nuclear branch. Neela and her sister seem as gently bred as others higher on the caste hierarchy, though some people still assume that their Patel background (referring to a less-prestigious portion of that caste than others) is an uneducated one. There are other families who come to call, hoping to make a match for their sons, who in fact do not have the same priorities as these parents. Hopes for their daughters clearly cannot rest on caste any longer, but must now rely on professionalism.[2] Neela's career orientation is a necessity; her parents want and need their daughters to have careers. This is not because the parents will be financially needy in their old age, despite Neela's vow to give them some of her money; they will have emotional needs, with no son to help supply them, and so they require their daughters to have some freedom of mind, some sense of personal agency. They must continue moving forward as members of a more generic educated urban middle class, and try to find educated, broad-minded husbands for their girls from

---

[2] Neela's family belongs to the Leva Patidars of Central Gujarat. This caste has a hierarchy of prestige within which this family's marriage circle is of a considerably lower rank. To aspire to marry either daughter into a higher rung, in which higher education more commonly prevails, would require a huge dowry and be prohibitively expensive, even though the father is a bank manager. In any case, such families are not choosing to call upon this family, as the story demonstrates.

within that pool. Appropriate matches will determine whether the daughters are happy, and whether the parents are happy as well. It is possible that they will have to go outside their caste find compatible partners for these two girls.

To sum up the gains and the losses, what Neela's mother has not had, she has made possible for her daughters; the loss of tight connections available to more observant caste members makes it possible for this family to live in a newer way; in all, the future looms ahead in an uncertain shape, which these parents are determined should be resolved happily.

Urmila in Mumbai is a striking example of confidence in one's identity, and of assertiveness as a realized capability. This strength of hers, however, uniquely supports a primary identity that does not approve of a bourgeois lifestyle, or equate female agency and autonomy with having ample amounts of money. Urmila will not make a lot of money in her profession, but she is excited with her ambition to be a teacher. She already is providing tuitions; she loves school children and they love her. She values family solidarity with a passion, not only in wanting to support her own parents, which she needs to do, but also in longing to remain tight with her whole community.

Urmila was 21 when I met her, a third year student toward her B.A. in sociology at a college affiliated with the University of Mumbai. She left a strong impression; she was radiantly joyful, with a ring to her voice; sure of herself and her plans for the future. She lives with her family in one of Mumbai's unique neighborhoods, where she has grown up. Her father is 53, educated up to SSC (10th standard). He works in a shop supplying uniforms and readymade garments for children, and has a slight disability. Her mother is 50, with her SSC, and is a housewife. The parents married at ages 25 and 22. The father's family is originally from Jamnagar; they are a Gujarati Vaishnav Bhatia family, worshippers of Krishna. When Urmila's father started working, his own father had died, and along with his older brother, he had two younger sisters to help support and get settled. Urmila's joint family now contains eight people, including her uncle and his family.

I am the youngest member of my joint family, and I have no siblings. For my career, I want to teach. Since my SSC I've been giving tuitions. I will take my B.Ed. exam in 2015, which qualifies me to teach up to 12th standard. Then I will get my M.Ed. I would have to get an M.A. as well to teach in a degree college, but I don't want to do that. I want to teach 5th through 10th standard. My parents have always wanted the best education for me. They gave me all the liberty to choose my own path. "Anything you do, you tell us," they say; "We'd appreciate knowing." I take tuitions and earn my own fees, so I do have some liberty. As soon as I get home from classes, I go straight upstairs to see my aunt, who's 56; we are so close, we even wear some of the same clothes. She always supports me if I'm right. She influences my mind even more than my parents, since she is elder. Her husband is 63; their son and his wife have a child. We all live together.

My mom says, "You should not be dependent on your husband, like we are." She did some cooking for dhabawallas earlier when there was a financial need, because my father's income is low. She made me get educated enough so I could earn after 10th standard. She questioned my plan to become a teacher, but my aunt explained it to her. In-laws would not have a problem with this career. They will think that going to office is too much mixing with men, and that teaching is more conservative. I'm not conservative—I just like teaching! I love giving tuitions.

Her family knew she had dated earlier, when she had a month-long relationship which was not serious. But she avows a strong dislike for love marriage. She exclaims,

I don't want to fall into love, and all that shit! I don't want a love marriage, even though my cousin and his wife have one, and my parents would allow it. I want to marry into the same caste, because I like my culture and religion. I go to church also. I pray at a Ganesha temple, and go to a gurdwara also to say a prayer. But I love my culture.

My married home can be either nuclear or joint, but I want my parents to find the husband. He should be older, taller and more educated than me. He should accept my parents as his parents, since mine have no son. We wouldn't live in the same house, but the way he would treat his parents, he should also treat mine. About money decisions, we should both make them together. There should be one salary for the household, and one for saving. My husband's income, if it's a bit more than mine, would be beneficial, but is not required. He should be honest, and he should respect my family. But from my income, there will be some part going to my parents. *I am their son.* I am already saving for my parents' old age, with returns to come after 25 years. I earn 8000 to 9000 rupees per month, which pays my fees, plus providing some to save. Next year, I won't ask a paisa for fees for my B.Ed.

On the first floor of our flat there is one room, on the second floor, two rooms. All eight of us live in the three rooms. I would like to give my children maybe a little more comfort, like today's generation; I'd like my kids to have their own room. I'd like to have at least one child, hopefully a girl, though a boy is good, too. I'll probably be with my in-laws for the kids. If there are no in-laws, my parents could take care, but only while I'm at work. Again, this is not the reason for choosing a teaching career. Kids like me so much! And I can do a lot with what I have—I don't need a luxurious standard of life. I don't want to be like rich people, who don't need their families. We are bonded with each other.

I'd love to do education in NGOs and with Teach for India while do-ing my B.Ed.—to help educate needy people, and people who do not understand that you should educate a girl child. My father's mother, 70 years ago, would have liked more education. Her children are all more educated.

Urmila struck me with her outspoken devotion not only to her family but also to her family's caste and religious affiliation. She carried this without any sense of contradiction, though I had met her in the class of her sociology teacher, a fire-breathing young feminist who leaves nothing unquestioned. Urmila did not come across as antifeminist; she was committed to the education of girls and the families of girls. However, as shown, she spoke fiercely about not believing in love marriage. She was anti-elitist, anti-consumerist, and anti-individual-ist. She was pro-children, in favor of loving and teaching them, in favor of continuing a lively relationship with her admired aunt, for supporting her parents just as a son would do, and for living in a very small house. She was in favor of prayer, wherever she might happen to practice it: in a church, in a gurdwara, at other temples, or at her own family shrine.

Urmila was also warmly in favor of women and girls. She had a conscious dignity as a committed daughter in being her parents' only child, planning on supporting them now, later, and in their old age. She wanted to have a daughter herself, if she were to have only one child. She wanted to get people who now fail to see it to believe in the need for girls to be educated. She was setting a steadfast example of a woman both becoming educated and providing education.

There is nothing new or unusual about Urmila's professional choice. Women have been teachers for decades, usually low-paid and undervalued, yet essential. But Urmila is also an upward riser, along with many of my other research subjects. Like Jaya, Vimla, and Vasanti, she wants to be part of the basic support of her parents and other family members, helping them reach an improved situation compared to the economic level they now inhabit, providing them with security, and making them proud. Her ambition is to attain the full professional standing available to an educated person so as to support her loved ones. Within this closely conjoined dual ambition, the professionalism she pursues is clear. She will fulfill her calling to teach children in standards 5 through 10, after obtaining educational qualifications entailing several degrees. She is given all the freedom that she wishes, what career to choose, whether to date or not, whether to marry by choice or not, whether to worship at different shrines, whom to see and where to go. She chooses to use this freedom to reinvest in the people she loves and lives with, eight people in three rooms.

What is the drawback? Her social field of vision is narrowly focused, outspokenly loyal to caste and community, which she calls her culture. Her entire apartment building is all of one caste. The reason she provides is a religious one: She says it is important to be a Vaishnav and a worshipper of Krishna living within a community of believers. Her religious sensibility is not exclusionary; her prayers at different worship locations speak to this. But her social circle is intensely protected, warding off any temptations to stray or to be forward or to meet someone with whom there might be a spark of passion. She seeks moral purity and personal commitment. Within this bastion of safety, she is powerfully confident.

Her commitment to teach public school may test her social boundaries in the future. The family she enters by way of marriage may challenge some of her notions, as well. It is fine-sounding to say that in-laws may be conservative, but that she is not; under these conditions, however, the likelihood that she too may need to become more conservative seems strong. She would like to serve children and her parents first and foremost; but once married, those commitments will be somewhat diluted by being joined with those owed to her new family.

The story represents some powerful gains. Urmila's sunny outlook and confident determination make it possible to imagine her standing on a podium, exhorting followers to do good. She is part of the legacy of ambition, growing far beyond her mother, leaning upon the more informed encouragement of her aunt. One wonders, however, whether the good she inspires in the future will be for people from every background. One can only hope, but not be sure, that her desire to promote women's equality will also be inclusive of a desire for equality among people of all communities.

Raina, in Allahabad, was 19, and in the first year of her B.A. program when we met. She plans to become a journalist. She is highly fluent in English, having attended a convent school where she specialized in debating. She is an opinionated, verbal, and self-consciously modern Muslim girl. She claims being Shia Muslim as her caste. When asked about her class location, she replied, "We are comfortably upper-middle class, I'd say."

> At home I have a younger brother, who's 16, and an older sister who is 23. My sister did her M.Com. and B.Ed., and now she's teaching at the inter-college level. My dad was one of seven, my mom one of four. My father is 55 and my mother is 47. She did her B.Ed. after graduation, but never taught. My father speaks English, but my mother doesn't. My father has training in management, and has worked in Qatar. He came back because my mother was having trouble handling three kids by herself. Now he has a shop here and one in Delhi. He has a manager in the one in Delhi, and goes there once or twice a month overnight by train.

I plan to be a journalist. I am willing to push ahead in it. Five to ten
years back, journalism was thought to be a profession only for boys.
When the Kargil war was going on, a female reporter named Khatab
was at the front, and the media was taking a lot of notice. Female
reporters are supposed to be exploited sexually, so families have objections. They expect daughters to write or sit in a studio, not to go
out to the front and interview people. Am I willing to do that, or not?
That was the first thing I talked with my parents about. My father
said, "Choose for yourself. But think it through, think of everything,
then take a decision and tell us." My mother was more hesitant. I told
them, "If I'm a journalist, I will do everything that a good journalist
would do. If you are not ready for that, tell me now, and I will choose
something else, because I don't want to disappoint you. If I become
a journalist and then you ask me to set limits, that won't work. It's
required that I go out. If I'm offered the assignment, I will go there."
So my parents see how serious I am. I must do what I am passionate
about. My mother knows she needs to be ready. I think my parents
are kind of exceptional.

This young woman displays some powerful gains, which now appear
more accessible than formerly to girls from wealthy but quite traditional families, whose own practices are sedate, yet who embrace
change for their children. She says,

I have some trouble with the atmosphere at the university. People
are not as broad thinkers here as they were in my school. I bond well
with boys; my best friends are two guy friends from inter-college.
Their college was next to mine. We were into debating, and used to
meet in competitions. I can debate anytime, anywhere.

Raina was very expressive. Every topic that came up she debated
from varied points of view. She was a wonderful talker. I sensed that
the great freedom her parents give her is based on their absolute trust
and confidence in her. I questioned, though, how she would eventually be able to carry out her mission. At 19 and only in her first year
toward the B.A., there were years for her to go before becoming, if
needed, a correspondent at the military frontier. That was not her
actual ambition as such; however, it was posed rhetorically as a limit-
ing factor in a debate with her parents. She actually imagined a career

that would ordinarily be more secure. "I plan to go into electronic media, and that way I can write for different newspapers more easily than if I start out working in print media. And I can work from home." She would like to have two or three children at most.

> I'd prefer two, but if my husband wants, I would be okay with three. I would not want just a single child. For each child, I should stay at home for at least one year. If my agency allows me, I'll work from home during that time. Journalism is like that. I will expect my husband to help out with the kids.

> In this generation I see a change in the guys as well as in the girls. I think they're getting there. Because of the restrictions their mothers are facing, they know that she has had limits. He is going to search for someone who is educated, who has had exposure. I can't say that I'll find a guy who's really liberal. They are trying to be adjusting, but it's not in their nature! They are trying to attain a modern guy image. They know they need to adjust, for their sisters as well, and not tell her what to do.

> It may not be fair if I do more of the housework (laughing), but I probably will. I'll be working alone in the house, so I can manage. I'll say, "I'm working as much as you are. I can cook, but at least you can set the dinner table." I'll appreciate if he cooks, but I love cooking. If I am managing well, it'll be nice if he offers sometimes. It'll be how he shows that he loves me! Women have to manage. Maybe after 7 or 8 years boys will have adjusted more. We'll see how they react to things we are asking, like: "Would you take some care of the kids?" Negotiation is a very important in a marriage, and in any relationship.

> If I find a boyfriend, I want him to be adjusting with me, just as much as I am adjusting to him. I'd say if this is not going as expected. He would not be happy with me as well, because I can't be a slave to someone. Emotionally we need to be good to each other.

Raina and I planned for me to visit her at home, but this never happened, because she did not return my later calls. She was so open and effervescent, and I asked so many questions, that after she told her mother about them, the openness seemed to shut down.

One of the drawbacks of a new way of life for women was pinpointed by Raina: the threat of a wife being forced to work against her wishes. She told me,

> Money is not so important, but a husband must be stable. My parents say, "If you are working, it helps out. But we don't want you to become an earning machine!" This is a new problem in India—where the wife has to earn. What if you want not to work? Or if you want to take a few years break? My sister plans to teach and then take a few years' break. You have the choice before marriage, whether you want to work or not. That should be the case after marriage as well.

The threat of being made into an "earning machine" plays into an existing pattern of treating women as means to an end, not in this case as daughters, but as wives. While men are expected to earn for their families, and might possibly complain of being treated instrumentally in that regard, the threat for women is potentially much more oppressive. To the extent that women are less valued in their families and communities compared to men, women can be dominated and subordinated in their marital families. Being forced to earn would simply be a variant form of that domination. In Raina's case, however, her own economic calculus needs to be examined as well. Raina does not want money to be used as a prime criterion in the selection of a husband. She also wants freedom not to work all the time, freedom to take a break for children, freedom not to be pressured. This presumes a marriage to someone who can provide income at the expected level.

Within her community, would it be likely for her parents (or for her, independently) to find the combination she desires, of both high earning and liberalism, in a husband and his family?

> Now the young are liberal; but the problem is to find a family that is liberal. The family should be open-minded. People in their 50s or 60s often have a problem if the young couple decides to move out and have their own space. They will say, "My son was so close to me, but now his wife is taking decisions. This is a betrayal. His wife has a duty to help us out."

Looking after parents in their old age had become the topic here; and she said, "We think of this often! We children say, 'Don't make your daughter-in-law stay with you all the time. There are three of us. We can care for you mutually. Your daughter-in-law needs vacations.' I'll say to my husband, allow me some time to be with my parents, too. But let's have all those discussions before the engagement!"

Suspicions about the full likelihood of her achieving the future she desires, and about the limitlessness of her family's allowances of freedom, were aroused by her saying, "Society is not yet comfortable with the idea of a girl being so open. Society is astonished by it. Other girls are amazed about my parents and what they are willing to adjust to."

We can be no more sure of any of these young women's being allowed or encouraged to continue on as professional workers after marriage than we can of most of the others, because we cannot predict what their in-laws will be like. This may somewhat depend upon these women setting conditions before marriage and being backed up by their parents in doing so.

Unborn Hopes

Most of the young women in this book have not considered either the challenge of continuing to grow in one's career after marriage, or the threat that holding onto that career may instead become a difficult chore. For example, women would need to grasp opportunities for on-the-job training, retraining, refining the tools of one's trade, upgrading one's skills, being promoted, and taking on more responsibilities. Some of these requirements may involve traveling out of town. Will these women be able to commit to these steps? These are all areas of professional life which are more likely to be familiar to girls who have well-educated career women for mothers. Women without this knowledge may not be in a strong position to negotiate for these steps either in planning their marriages, or within their marital families.

Career women who are mothers understand a number of other things that mothers who do not work have little idea about. If the career mothers of today had to do it again, some might not choose to marry the same husband they settled down with. They may wish they had found more compatibility and emotional support, if they have been juggling all their roles without anyone in the family appreciating their challenges or regarding the career itself with respect. The mothers of the girls in my sample are agreeable about their daughters' demands for careers. But mothers who have not had occasion to contemplate the challenges of professionalism may be less able to advise their daughters on how to combine career and marriage, or even on whom to consider marrying.

A few of my research subjects have the idea that a couple ought to be compatible in having similar professional interests. They do not imagine the competition this could lead to, with the husband laying claim to greater prestige or higher earning. Current middle-aged career women with successful marriages have dealt with such issues with the help of their husbands, via good communication and mutual compromise. If a woman is to thrive in her career as she would like to, she needs a partner who has an interest in her goals and passions, whom she can talk with. It could be easier to find this kind of compatibility without having a marriage arrangement that is based on caste, if career mothers and fathers arranged introductions based on compatibility and mutual professional commitment among friends across a spectrum of educated careers. If parents consider the professional and intellectual interests of the young people involved, rather than being primarily committed to caste networks, more productive matches may be possible than if confined within those networks.

Whatever criteria are used for selecting a marriage partner, however, there is no real protection against a woman being dominated and disrespected by a husband or his family. The ideal conditions with all the relatives who live together may also not be found in a particular family that a girl marries into. Getting the marital family to cooperate so that a young woman's professionalism can grow and flower may require a protracted struggle for respect. Even given a kindly family and cooperative relatives, some career-focused hopes may fall apart because the coverage of household needs in a particular family situation cannot be complete without the wife sacrificing her career.

A professional identity is more than simply having a job as a source of employment. A profession is seen as a kind of service requiring the use of one's moral and intellectual resources. A woman bent on a professional identity needs both a love for her career choice, and the full capability to pursue it, so she can fulfill her commitment to developing it to its best.

The Mothers Left Behind

In seeing family histories as social history, recapturing the female mores of the previous generation is important in establishing changes in gender expectations that are now taking place. Here I give attention to the mothers of the research subjects. Three mothers whom I met were described in detail: Shruti's, Tanika's, and Neela's.[3] The enthusiastic attitudes of the mothers of Jaya, Vimla, and Tamara I experienced in person; what Rita shared allowed me to describe her mother's painful conundrum. Other mothers appeared only through the interview with the daughter. There are several young women whose own stories have not been used in the book, yet whose mothers' part in them is useful to consider. I order these stories here from the well-educated non-working mothers in well-to-do homes, to the less educated and poorer mothers.

A young woman living in a wealthy home in Vadodara told me of her ambitious plans. Her mother, a housewife with a college degree, was ill and in pain, and wanted her help with household work. There was plenty of money, but the mother refused to ask her prosperous husband to hire a maid. She was self-denying, insisting that outsiders could not do the work correctly. The younger sister, not as ambitious as my subject, was closer to the mother and helped her, while my subject was closer to her father and focused on her studies.

One non-working mother with an M.A. had a love marriage; the father had taught her in secondary school. This mother has two daughters, and insisted on having both girls educated at a convent school.

---

[3]   In Chapter 5, Chapters 2 and 6, and Chapter 7, respectively.

She supported them in extra activities such as art, sketching, and dance. This mother now says she'd like to be a primary school teacher.

A Mumbai college girl's long-term boyfriend had recently been killed in a motorcycle accident. Her mother was pushing her to start looking again for a mate. This girl, who is from a Christian family, will not have an arranged marriage, and her family expects her to choose a mate as well as to establish a career. She says, "My mother wants me to complete my degree, because she couldn't finish college. She expects a lot of me!" My subject feels the pressure.

A young woman from Rajasthan lives with her younger sister in Mumbai, where both are studying. They live on their own in an apartment. Their mother, who grew up in Mumbai, finished 12th standard, but her in-laws did not allow her to continue. My subject's family had lived in Mumbai, but then moved to Rajasthan, where the father now has a business. The mother has five children, the other three younger than the two college girls. The mother feels very tied down at home. She wants more freedom and to travel the world. My subject says, "The only thing that matters is what my parents think of me. They are proud of us, my mother especially. My mother's idea is different than her mother's. She says, 'Always take a stand. We know you are right.' She puts up with a lot." This daughter wants to make her mother happy more than she wants to marry anyone.

A Vadodara student says, "My family is totally supportive, but finances are not so good." Her mother finished 12th standard, and did not take a low-prestige job when the husband's business affairs went through a crippling low point; but my subject's older sister took a temporary job in a call center to help. This younger sister says, "I need to work and earn for the family for two years. After marriage, I want to give some of my earnings to my parents. My mother tells me, 'You must become independent. Culture and tradition are changing now.'" This was ironic, in that the mother had refused to work when more income was needed.

A student in Mumbai has parents who knew each other from childhood, living in different apartments in the same building. It was a love marriage, but in the same caste. Her mother finished only 10th standard. "Even now, she wishes she had studied further. Now she's trying to learn English, and we help her."

A student planning to do her M.A. lives with her divorced mother. She is the only child of parents who had a love marriage, coming from different regions. The mother is uneducated, but can read. She supports her daughter's career, wants her to find her own mate, and gives her complete freedom to go out and date. The daughter will be supporting her mother.

Another Mumbai student says, "My Mom wishes she'd had more education, especially English. She feels that if she were more educated, she could have earned for the family too. She even has to ask her kids to dial through the name list on her mobile."

A girl in Allahabad says, "My mother is a good housewife, who sacrifices everything for me and my sister." The two girls feel ardently bound to help support their parents.

Most of these mothers feel that they are missing out in some important way. They exist on the cusp of gender change, but have not either had any chance or taken any risks to participate in it. Their own mothers followed even more rigid customs. Seeing this helps these mothers to justify putting heavy expectations on their daughters. An exception is the mother who focused on her girls' schooling and extracurricular activities, and now feels life is still ahead of her so she can seek a late primary school teaching career. On the other hand, the educated mother who is unwell and yet so possessive of her housework is to be pitied, while her claims on her daughters seem self-indulgent. The mother who wants her daughter to hurry and find a mate while she is still grieving seems very insensitive. The Mumbai-raised mother feeling trapped in Rajasthan and now looking to her eldest children, both daughters, for any pleasure that life may afford her, has made her firstborn (at least temporarily) disdain marriage altogether.

Two themes are shown in the messages these mothers seem to be sending to their daughters. One is, "What I never was allowed to have, I want for you." The other is, "I want you not only to support yourself, but also to give things to me that I need." Of the two messages, one may be stressed more, but often they coincide. Most of the excerpts show the combination clearly. The messages are filtered through each young woman's consciousness as revealed in her narration. Each of my subjects is keenly aware that she owes her mother not only love but also duty; that she is important to her mother not only for emotional reasons but probably for providing goods and services, too. From a weak position, these mothers exert undeniable power over their daughters.

The feminine role of caring is overemphasized in these messages the daughters are hearing from their mothers. Their fealty to family grips them while they study and aspire. Even as they wish to make their parents proud, they sense the sacrifices and losses their mothers have sustained. Priya in Vadodara spoke of her mother's faithfully carrying out all the correct behaviors required in a Rajasthani family, always covering her head in front of male family members, while the other members of Priya's nuclear unit (her father, her sisters, and she) are forging ahead in work and study in a more progressive vein. Part of daughters' responses to their mothers' life situations is pure sympathy. Partly they respond with a sense of obligation.

The self-identity sought by these young women, the first in their families to seek professional careers, is of a kind that keeps them firmly identified *with* their families. Their sense of self-identity is non-individualistic; their personal agency operates within the circle of affection, loyalty, and responsibility shared with their families. These optimistic young women are deeply embedded in families, committed to making their families happy as well as themselves. They are not bent on separating and building a new life on their own; they are aiming at blending the generations as harmoniously as Indian tradition desires, but in a new pattern. They did not come up with this new vision entirely on their own; it has been their parents' as well.

Once young women are married, however excellent their education and career preparation has been, however high their hopes, and however carefully they have selected their marital family, stereotypical gender roles may reassert themselves, due to expectations by husbands and mothers-in-law that men will not have to pick up too many parts of the domestic duties (Mukhopadhyay and Sudarshan 2003: 117). However, some of these women will probably attain a middle-class status in which they are able to afford the domestic help that they will require. A changing and evolving class hierarchy will thus help sustain a lifestyle that challenges the gender hierarchy pertaining to the more elevated class. This is not an irony; it is a perfect fit, a logical outcome—a class formation outcome (well noted also in Fernandes 2006).

Embeddedness and Economic Pressure

In looking at embedded agency, the research reported here relates closely to that of Saavala (2010), Waldron (2012), Radhakrishnan (2011), Roy (2014), and others. These works all employ a generous narrative interview methodology, bringing the interviewer close to the subject's life world, challenges, and negotiation strategies. The highly embedded agency of women is a theme in all these current-day works for the precise reason that families still rule the roost. As Roy (2014) writes, however, a woman's "agency is at once embedded and transformative. That is, agency and resistance can be seen as occurring within the locus of power relations and not in some 'pure' space outside of power" (2014: 175).

Being embedded has a more outward set of outcomes too. As the pressure-cooker of the almost unregulated capitalist world system has reached into every corner of the globe, parenting a daughter to move into a professional environment and succeed is a new response. A close parent–daughter bond is required to make it work. An implied understanding of a continuing long-term relationship partly takes the place of the traditional obligations that weaken continuing relations of parents with their daughters. What we are seeing now, however, is simply a newer way for families to deploy their members so as to ensure the well-being of the family as a whole. Education plays the role of helping a family deploy its children into economic sectors that require that education. What is changed is the manner of deployment of *daughters*.

The emerging globalized employment picture of the last few decades has been more than the young women's parents could have fully imagined back in the 1980s and 1990s, when their children were being born. Given these circumstances, however, parents reap benefits from having invested in their daughters' education and relative freedom. Their experience in doing so sets an example for later parents to consider. This may be helping lead to modifications in gender expectations among other people, who are just beginning to sense an opportunity in having young adult daughters at home for more years. Such groups of people may be not only urban but also even semi-rural, wherever parents are able to educate their daughters up to secondary level with a good knowledge of English, and to see them enter college. A sense of new opportunities for girls, new reasons for daughters to be valued, thus penetrates into new layers of the country.

Education, urbanization, globalized labor market shifts, and rapid fertility decline, along with population pressure and tight economic competition, all work together to delineate newly envisioned family survival strategies. The practice of deploying members of the family to help the group, though it changes in some of its details, does not disappear. Daughters may stay at home, or within the orbit of the natal family, longer, providing benefits to natal families as well as to those into which they marry. What will probably spread far and wide will be the hope of girls to become persons of greater respect, not only out in the wide world, but also within the confines of their own families.

8

Social Reproduction and the Professional Imaginary

Some young women are now seeking self-identities that they did not or could not seek before. A newly created kind of female self seems to be appearing out of backgrounds where the same could not flourish earlier. In this chapter, I plan to establish how this newness (rare and special though its occurrence may still be) stems from aspirational families encouraging their daughters to take up careers, and how at the same time it is about deeper underlying socioeconomic forces.

First, we look back at the young women whose stories have been considered, in light of a growing professional imaginary which has caught hold of them. This phenomenon characterizes women located in both the old and new middle classes, and therefore we briefly examine various approaches to the development of middle-class identities. The chapter then turns to a consideration of social reproduction as it begins to undergo systemic change. Finally, it undertakes to draw a picture of the emerging form of self-identity that is being shaped and molded by young urban women, and to imagine some of the implications of this development for the future for women.

The Genealogy of Women's Ambition

Living in India in the late 1960s and 1970s, I experienced the palpable gap that existed in the genealogy of ambition and career aspiration among educated women. I was acquainted with well-educated women who are members of the mother and grandmother generations of today's college women; and being college-educated back then meant, almost inevitably, that they were of elite and upper-caste background. If they worked outside the home, it was often due to family reverses and a resolve to maintain a middle-class level of support. Of course, those who sought PhDs and other highly advanced professional degree qualifications were quite different. But many women in the urban middle-class families I knew, though well-educated, became solely housewives after marriage and never seriously entertained other plans. Such families could unquestioningly educate daughters up to the Master's level, and still have them settle down to immediate marriage and housewifery. In this new era, one can bridge that genealogical gap by looking at women whose mothers, even if well-educated, have not worked; daughters who themselves are now articulately seeking lifetime professional careers. Today's aspirers, in addition, encompass new people, members of a newly rising part of the middle class. These include young women not coming from upper-caste or upper-class backgrounds, whose mothers have very little education.

The students in this project speak English and are studying for careers in the medium of the English language. One of their favorite words is "exposure," by which they mean global awareness. The women of this new generation are connected with a wider world via saturated media and communications technology. It is important not to overstate the global transparency of these connections, because for many, the globalized mirror they look into does not have a very clear or accurate view of other countries and regions of the world. Its images are refracted through certain hopes and various prejudices. But this mirror does reflect back to them the upward climb of women. Which of the women of the world and of India are not enjoying any such rise is a question that must be kept always in mind.

But with global exposure, increased by the Internet, a highly visible swath of women globally can be seen as growing more powerful.

Studying the lives and hopes of middle-class and would-be middle-class women is richly worthwhile for perspectives both including but also broader than feminism. The growing embourgeoisement of ordinary folk in India today has a long tail of history. Reaching back into the 19th and early 20th centuries, the thrust of common rural life was powerfully to gather the people into villages and castes and communities. The forward tendencies of urban life were to organize working people, consolidate business interests, and develop strong institutions under a colonial and later a national umbrella. These were patriarchal projects, which in fact greatly increased male dominance while centralizing communities further under that dominance. In a historical context, the growth and expansion of the urban middle class in India today is rather different. More encompassing and far-reaching than was ever before imagined, part of its newness is in holding more possibilities for women to have more complex lives and identities.

The historical overview sketched above is selective in saying little of nationalism, anti-imperialism, or religious sectarianism. There is an impetus toward forming and shaping oneself as a person—toward becoming a "bourgeoise" of one's own, so to speak—that is driven by demographic and economic change more than, yet leading the way for, cultural and political change. Until the 1980s, due in part to high mortality and fertility combined with slow economic growth, India was unable to diversify its economy sufficiently to produce a slate of new opportunities for a great many more people. It then began to do so alongside much news about nationalism and religious sectarianism, trends which continue to gather ominous strength. In fact, there has been no phase of Indian history since 1800 and well before, without some trace, large or small—sometimes hidden—of such tendencies and the fearsome conflicts they can engender. What has been very new, however, has been rapid economic development, which kept up a pace outstripping that of many other nations from about 1993 to 2008, and then slowed down. Fifteen years of high-speed development, followed by a global slowdown, has been the result of the greater global integration of this period.

This recent slowdown and halting recovery places many young educated middle-class and newly middle-class women in a critical position. They want professional jobs, just like their male peers, and they want both supportive and well-employed husbands. The men they are introduced to mainly want employed wives. A member of the couple needs to be well employed, preferably both; it will usually not be only the wife, unless a state of affairs considered most undesirable comes to pass within a particular marriage. Women's jobs are more expendable than men's, and men's employment has remained a reliable mainstay under unquestioned patriarchal conditions. It may remain so; or it may begin to be undermined.

Professionalism

Professionalism is an elastic, renewable, and multipliable category, very useful to assess at this global juncture. It is also an important factor to be considered in the making of self-identity. The discussion of professions in this research has been limited to those roles that require a college education or better. These roles have broadened and multiplied in recent times. Since the late 1980s, India began to produce newer and more varied career opportunities for more of its educated people of both sexes and diverse backgrounds. The broad unemployment situation referenced in earlier chapters is a serious challenge, but within employment, there are more choices and more roles to play, given the talent, the skill, and the training for the particular job opportunity and being in the right place to find it. Urban centers are by far the best hope for educated careers, though expanded roles also exist in rural management in private firms, government jobs, and nongovernmental organizations.

Professionalism ought to be considered as something more than the holding of a certificate and winning of a job by that means. Aiming to provide a glimpse into career-minded women's growing sense of self-identity, it is clear that professionalization is a rich part of that process. How a fully professional self-identity is formed and arrived at, and then tenaciously held throughout a life, will be a major challenge facing my research subjects.[1] It involves a lifelong task of commitment to increasing one's skill development, set of accomplishments, and professional advancement. This task has been carried out by all of my colleagues—professors, writers, activists—who almost all started out with certain advantages. Today's young career aspirants may or may not start out with social advantages. They may or may not seek careers that are very lucrative. But they are looking for meaningful lives, wanting careers that provide service, employ knowledge, attain respect and dignity, and hold a kernel of moral force, as well.

In expanding on how new roles offer chances for women to create new kinds of self-identities, I offer the case of an aspiring archaeologist, *Amrita*, at the Maharaja Sayajirao University in Vadodara. (Kusum, in the same department, appeared in Chapter 4). Amrita's story is one that shows a particularly huge leap in self-identity, assertiveness, freedom, and agency between mother and daughter. She is 21 and in her first year for the M.A. in fine arts—museology. She has her B.A. in archaeology and wants to become a curator in an archaeological museum. The nearby Baroda Museum[2] has an archaeological section, and the Maharaja Sayajirao University's Department of Museology has its own museum with valuable ancient pieces in it, so the stimuli here are very rich.

Amrita says, "I selected archaeology out of interest. On a school field trip, I saw signboards at sites we visited, and looked up the word on the internet. My parents said, 'Select your field as you like. But you must make a career in that field.'"

This way of finding out what one is interested in is completely contemporary, stemming from the availability of the Internet and the World Wide Web. This is "exposure" in a seamless manner, and also real choice. The wide world of careers is at one's doorstep to choose from, given the flexibility of one's parents. Amrita's parents are startlingly flexible, stemming from a conservative background.

---

[1] Poonacha and Gopal (2004) provide an excellent analysis of lifelong issues facing the careers of professional women in science.

[2] The museum's name is unchanged from its old form.

They allow her to study whatever she likes, and she has been attracted to the arts. Her mother is very artistic, but not highly educated. The parents only say that in choosing what to study, she should find a vocation and then follow it.

> My mother is dependent, and has to ask for money. She finished 10th standard in her village near Porbandar. My father has a degree, and has worked in finance; he's now retired. My parents live in Baroda now. For my 11th and 12th, I was boarding in Mumbai, living in a hostel. In my Bachelors here, my subjects were French, Archaeology, and Travel and Tourism. My brother says many around here are now learning French, going in for tourism opportunities.

> Obviously, I will choose my own husband if I marry. Our caste is Hindu general category; an inter-caste marriage would be okay, and there's no rule about what age to marry. But I don't want to marry! I want to live my life as I do right now. My mother says it's fine if you don't want to marry. My initial salary would be no more than 10 thousand per month; I'd live with my parents if possible, or find a place as a paying guest, or an apartment with others. I don't want to lose my freedom or my career. Here you have to choose between child and career. Better not to get married than face all the complications.

> My mother has always wanted me to have a career. She did want a career, but as a girl, her parents did not encourage the idea. She is good at fine arts and embroidery, and she designs these traditional things that I wear.

> I will get a job anywhere in the country. I like teaching; and one can be an educator in museums, too. To pursue my career, if I find I need a Ph.D., I will do it.

> Professionalism is being well trained and working in a field you are trained in. It means specialization. Professional behavior in the workplace means fulfilling your duties, respecting your job, being acknowledged and vice versa. You must grab your opportunities. I can speak up about things I'm determined to do.

Amrita gives voice to almost the greatest possible freedom and latitude found among the college women I met. She is already living a life that she loves and being the person she wants to be. She has a well fleshed-out conception of professionalism, the moral core of it and the drive to grow in it. She is free to choose her marital or single state. Her parents are transition people, traditionally rooted in conservative Porbandar, but with the shift in perspective that has become possible from living in Vadodara. If Amrita finds a not very high-paying job in her field that allows her to live at home, they would probably encourage her to stay there, enjoying the newness of this shifted perspective of being an ongoing nuclear family that includes a son interested in things global and a daughter interested in things artistic and historical.

Let me now review patterns found in the stories I have told, offering thoughts about both the fitness and the capabilities of each young woman to become a full-fledged professional. This provides background to a discussion of what I call the professional imaginary. The "capability" for each one to succeed identified in these vignettes closely follows a part of the usage of that word suggested by Sen, in falling within the frame of the young woman's broader circumstances. Almost every woman interviewed possesses a realized "assertiveness capability" that well outstrips that of her mother. The question is whether each one is likely to have the "circumstantial capability" to succeed in becoming fully professional. After reviewing these cases, we will further discuss this distinction in capabilities that I have just pointed to.

In Chapter 4, a group of seven students appeared. Rita, in Allahabad, hopes to find employment in the National Rural Health Mission, doing work that advances causes for rural women. She may rise in her organization to a position of leadership and decision-making power. Whether or not these agencies offer her such ranks, if she works for some years and then opens her own NGO for women's empowerment, as she intends, she will be the leader and decision maker. These roles will be crucial in professionalizing her.

Shyamili, in Bengaluru, will rely on her networks to advance. Through her graduate school program, she has the "forward linkages" referred to by Sahni and Shankar (2012). If she succeeds in becoming employed using her MBA-equivalent degree, she will feel that she is among the ranks of professionals. Some MBAs, however, end up in what ought to be considered working-class roles in call centers and BPO companies in Bengaluru, even if rather well-paid ones. She has expectations of a prosperous marriage, and may not remain committed to a career if hers does not prove a promising one.

Kusum (like Amrita) may become a museum curator, though jobs are few and far between. She may settle in a small, out-of-the-way place. Such jobs are certainly considered professional, though they may not carry growth potential unless one becomes the museum's director. Kusum hopes for a husband with a similar career; such a couple would earn very little between them. If her romantic scheme of marriage to a museum colleague comes true, her husband might get preferment in promotion due to gender discrimination, and she might find that her work is considered secondary.

Sonam, in Mumbai, will be a person of influence, either in Nagpur or the smaller town nearby where her fiancé is settled, because of her dynamic personality, her firm grasp of skills and options, and her experience as a student leader. She will make decisions and make things happen, either together with her intended husband, or on her own. She wants to start a training business. If she succeeds in starting a company where she trains and mobilizes employees, she can forge herself into a professional trainer without obtaining further formal qualifications. She has the support of her family and of her self-chosen fiancé.

Abhita, in Vadodara, has the opportunity to become a professor in her own department, based on her unique research and the enthusiasm of her senior colleagues for it. Being a professor is by its original definition a professional rank; but her own ambition is muted and modest so far, not driven by a sense of insistent personal requirement. Her staying employed there is a matter of what her in-laws may choose; and who they will be depends on her parents and what choices they can discover within the Soni caste community.

Rani, in Mumbai, is of two minds about working after marriage. She has professional-level knowledge about extension education and rural outreach, which she shares enthusiastically. But her motivation for working is based on wanting not to be bored, far from a professional commitment. And the profession she is becoming qualified for is located rurally, while her parents and her future marital family will probably manage to keep her in Mumbai. She might switch professional aims and become successful in new ones; she is articulate and strong.

Priya, in Vadodara, seems very promising to succeed. She does unique research and has a resume of relevant experience already. Her father is trying to make it possible for her to fulfill her career potential by searching for a broad-minded marital family. Once she completes her research project and gets hired in her department to teach, she has the decisive personal attributes and knowledge to become highly professional, both as a faculty member and as a business woman. Her chance to remain an active professional may depend upon her mate.

In Chapter 5, we met some young women from families who urgently need their daughters to work at a level providing them with both income and dignity, in contrast with others from more elite and prosperous locations. Jaya, in Allahabad, at 17, is a bright, idealistic young person desiring to become an IAS officer, studying at the university which produces a great many of them. Finding IAS officers serving with integrity is not guaranteed, though they are classed as professional. It would be her intention to carry out her role with idealism; and her parents would support her career, which would continue to benefit them socially as well as financially.

Sarita, from Pondicherry, whom I met in Bengaluru, was moving toward higher-level employment than her BPO job by doing a night course on human resource (HR) management. HR is a role that is not always treated as a truly professional one in many companies. It is under the thumb of one or more of the other chief officers in most, and has little access to decision-making; yet it is one of the occupations that are considered professional. Sarita's family is eager for her to have a dignified career.

Vimla, in Allahabad, is hedged about by controls imposed by her proud father (perhaps out of sheer necessity). Well versed in philosophy and feminist theory, her professionalism as a knowledge agent and a teacher is already fully in place. She has great force of character; but problems seem to rise before her like impenetrable boulders. Can a woman with a strong feminist philosophy but limited permission to move freely find a supportive mate coming from her faction-riven community? Her full professionalization will depend upon it.

Vimla's interview had reminded me of Kamayani and Revathi in Bengaluru. Kamayani, despite her wishes and her winning ways, would likely not be allowed to become a professional. She was being allowed to earn money before marriage within the confines of a decisively conservative family network. Revathi, by contrast, will probably succeed in attaining her goal of becoming the legal advisor to a company, a professional role and identity far beyond anything achieved or imagined by her parents. (Her younger sister was opting out altogether, though with an architecture degree she may yet find professional-level work.) Revathi is fully supported in her goals by her husband, as she has been by her parents.

Vasanti, in Mumbai, setting out to support her parents and younger sisters by working in marketing for large companies, will surely succeed; her last employer promised to get her placed in whatever company she chose upon her graduation. She has proved herself, and it was clearly seen that she deserved sponsorship. Working just in marketing might or might not allow her to develop as a professional, but rising in the ranks to a director level would provide that opportunity. The mutual commitment between her and her parents seems inviolable.

The story of Shruti in Allahabad is an example of a girl who comes from an elite background and has the drive, talent, knowledge, and backing to reach an outstanding professional place. It is one that is unusual and only recently growing in Allahabad, the role of a female advocate. A lawyer, like a professor, is in an a priori professional category. She has an important ally in her father, who also can provide the networks she will need.

In Chapter 6, we met Tanika and Tamara, privileged in contrasting ways, yet enjoying generations of advantage in the genealogy of female ambition. Both Brahmin in caste, they each also have individual qualities required of professional people even further along in careers than they are. The confidence, style, and knowledge they display, idealistically placed in service to education and justice, are convincing reflections of their long-standing cultural capital. Their careers will surely further the cultural pride of their families.

In Chapter 7, we met Neela, Urmila, and Raina. Neela has elegance, fluent English, and design talent. Through her artistic abilities, she is likely to fit into a fashion niche that is called professional in today's terminology. Urmila will without question be a professional as a schoolteacher, though not with the glossy kind of professionalism that much of today's generation wants to attain. Both these young women clearly enjoy their parents' approval and support. Raina is a brilliant girl aiming to be an adventurous journalist, most certainly a professional category. Her community may not encourage her, although her parents do.

The assertiveness capability that most of these women possess is a strength that will redound to their benefit if their circumstances do permit them to begin their careers. This will depend to a considerable degree on other people's demands on them. But with the assertiveness they have developed, and have been encouraged to develop, most will continue to make their own demands on others to a much larger extent than their mothers did. If they find a place in the work world, they will be much more likely to hold on to it and develop it further. The circumstantial capability to do so may be buttressed by supportive husbands and in-laws, who are much more likely to appear in their lives than was the case for the previous generation.

The Professional Imaginary

There are several different kinds of professionalism dealt with here. The notion originally pertained to the traditional professions: law, medicine, the clergy, and academia, as well as government, diplomacy, and the military, in which top ranks were recognized for centuries. Engineering, business management, and accounting have long since been added to that classical list: these are prestigious, demanding, highly paid careers, accessed through education with rigorous entry criteria for required postgraduate degree studies. There are now, however, many more ranks and levels within business and organizational structures that require professional qualifications, HR, for example.

There is also a more current, less elevated notion of professions, which refers to any career informed by specific training and educational preparation. These are now marked by certificates and new degree programs, which multiply by the decade. More and more occupations are requiring certificates. This trend allows increasingly more elementary levels of service work, nonprofit work, business services, health care, teaching, training, and personal care to be considered professional. For instance, one can become a professional masseur. The professions enumerated under either the classical definition and the more recent ones are visualized as providing services to persons, organizations, the state, or the wider community in one way or another. The term is also applied to entertainment and to sports.

Currently, in addition to all of the above, we see the spread of the word "professional" as a descriptor of lifestyle characteristics seen as both modern and middle class. To give an example, one can be told in seeking accommodation that a particular hostelry is (or is not) known as a "professional-level" hotel, even if one is just a traveler, not looking for a conference center.[3] There can be some levity in such usage, while other examples actually denote greater dignity for people doing particular jobs. For example, one sees waiters and servers in neat but not fancy uniforms, serving in restaurants and hotels, many of whom have been to hotel management schools and obtained certificates. The "professionalism" seen in the broad expansion of this word is of an aspirational kind, relating partly to increased credentialism imposed from above (see Fernandes 2006), and partly to the seeking for personal dignity and social inclusion that people wish to have attributed to themselves.

Radhakrishnan's *Appropriately Indian* (2011) identifies a transnational class of Indian professionals, a much higher status level of families than those chosen for this book, but representing the highest levels of professionalism. She finds even among women at that level a conflicted consciousness, casting a partial shadow over their pride in achieving their professional goals. She gives an example of a woman who proudly plays the role of career-driven breadwinner in her family, but who at the same time "find[s] it difficult to

---

[3] For a relevant consideration of contemporary real estate development and the image of the professional, see Searle 2013.

enact respectable femininity" in her everyday life (2011: 154). She writes, "Professional women draw upon deeply resonant notions of the family, even as they reconcile those meanings with notions of individual achievement imbibed from the workplace" (2011: 148).[4]

The urban middle-class professional imaginary as applied to women is heavily tied in with a continued insistence upon family and community. The careers of its children are a family's project, just as much as their marriages are. The daughters we are discussing are projected to succeed on both fronts, each of which contributes to the welfare and prestige of the family. Within the professional imaginary of most of these young urban women themselves, there is a hope for a future that encompasses a carefully calibrated compounding of professionalism and marriage. The vision is for a woman to obtain one or more degrees, begin her career, and then marry later than women of an earlier generation did. In this life plan, the years of educational preparation should ideally not be followed immediately by marriage. As Shruti says, "I want to go through a phase when I'm not married, where I'm into my career and am not all that much monitored."

Hovering over some of my other research subjects is a veiled desire to have some time of one's own, along with doubts that there can be much of it. For example, here is Abhita saying, "I probably should marry by age 25. But right now, I have time to explore my career." Priya is imploring her father to fend off conservative relatives in Rajasthan, while she staffs and directs her own showroom and does university research, having already reached the ripe age of 25. Two young women from village families, Rita (Chapter 4) and Vimla (Chapter 5), both urgently need, before they can get married, to work and support their younger brothers so their families will have college-educated sons to support them. This gives them some leverage with their families, if not the liberty to live as they wish.

"Despite the façade of rapid social change, the major undercurrent of social relatedness among middle class people still centres on the hierarchies of kin" (Saavala 2010: 88). In the expanding

---

[4] Radhakrishnan's findings in Bangalore in this regard are very like those recently found in New York City by Damaske (2011), who shows how employed women there insist on justifying their work as being all for the family.

professional imaginary of these families, a young educated woman may tacitly wish for a little space of her own before marriage, but much more clearly, she envisions a hoped-for refuge within her marriage. This is the vision that carries her forward: a marriage will be contracted with a man who is egalitarian and helpful, highly qualified and well settled. His parents will be extremely compliant with having a daughter-in-law whose career keeps her away from household duties most of each day. They will happily cooperate in helping care for the children and in making life easier for the couple. This is the set of requirements that appears to be the sine qua non for her career to thrive.

There can be a more frankly feminist professional imaginary, which sorts more uneasily with the growing middle-class professional imaginary. It involves pushing forward the boundary of women's rights, and claiming one's own rights as such. But in the interviews on which I have reported, few young women see themselves claiming all the rights enumerated in the Universal Declaration of Human Rights (United Nations, 1948). For example, Article 17 guarantees the right to own property and not to be arbitrarily deprived of it: and there could be professional advancement and/or business startup funds to be found by owning one's birthright. But few girls who have brothers want to hold out for their share of the family property.[5] They most vehemently agree with Article 3, however, which guarantees life, liberty, and security of person to all people, and thus stands as an ideological bulwark against rape, and supports women's freedom to move around just as freely and safely in public spaces as men.

If women become successfully employed, they can advocate for women from within the organizations they work for. If they become entrepreneurs, they can set the terms of equality within their own firms and NGOs. Even if they do not find what they seek in the workplace, and are obliged to accept lesser jobs or work in unsatisfying arrangements, they will still remain charged with a sense of

---

[5] My thanks for this perspective go to a group of Allahabad law students, for whom I facilitated a group discussion on these articles at their service club meeting. I later tested this notion with of several other groups at different locations. In terms of what women students were willing to say in public, the finding was the same.

possibility, which, like their forebears, they will pass on to their own daughters and sons, nieces and nephews, students they tutor, people they volunteer with, neighbors, and friends. And whether even employed or not, they may seek in their own ways to become activists for women. Or, they may become satisfied with their superiority and exploitive of others less well qualified, reinforcing the fetters of the class system that is emerging, with some of its roots located in the caste hierarchy. This possibility cross-cuts the progress we see.

Middle-class Identity

There is a growing academic interest in the burgeoning middle class in India. Numerous seminars have been examining the subject in the past few years (e.g., Baviskar and Ray 2011). Though the term "middle class" has been in use in India since the 19th century, it was then a somewhat notional label for a tiny English-educated elite. "Paradoxically, in striking contrast with the English middle classes, the emergent Indian educated 'middle class' was rooted primarily in rent income from land, where production relations were far from capitalistic ... combined with professions and office jobs in government or European business firms" (Sarkar and Sarkar 2007: 2). This privileged combination placed it squarely in an elite, upper-caste category. The basis of today's growing middle class is more accurately based just on the professions, white collar employment, and business. We will locate it shortly in economic terms.

However, it is currently being actively discussed as a cultural formation. Fernandes (2006) refers to the rise of what is being called a "new" middle class as "a cultural and a normative political project, because it helps shape the terms of development and national identity." In regard to middle-class *identity,* then, some well-regarded works place special emphasis on the process of keeping up appearances. Describing weddings and other consumerist and leisure practices, Brosius (2010) writes, "the new middle classes in India depend on visibility, visuality and performativity" (2010: 24). Saavala's 2010 study of women in Hyderabad who are climbing toward the middle class emphasizes the social formalities they learn to conform to and the rituals they learn to perform, reinforcing the performative aspect of class that Brosius highlights. Referring to the political agitation behind urban beautification and cleansing programs, Fernandes (2006) identifies what she calls a "spatialized production of middle-class identity" (2006: 137).

Middle-class aspirations are thus seen to be shaped around consumerism and geared toward appearances and political one-upsmanship. These authors among others view this kind of consumerism as being quite effective in helping whole groups make new cultural or political claims. Such writings put forward an understanding of the middle class which then can appear as a scrim of cultural and political construction, floating visibly on top of a seething mass of economic and personal struggle. Performativity, as seen in the writings of authors cited above, can sometimes seem almost to congeal a person's actions and limit her freedom of choice about how to think.

In regards to both social constraints and the development of a reflective self-identity, Bourdieu's ideas are relevant to consider. In his framework, "symbolic systems are instruments of domination" (Jain 2006: 105), which explain women's subordination under the direction of their inner habitus. Thapan (2006), however, finds in Bourdieu a space for consciousness, thinking, and resistance, identifying "multiple subjectivities" (2006: 203) that women can navigate to their own advantage, allowing them to resist oppressive circumstances, even if only inwardly.

Seeing class behavior in terms of appearances may in fact be a reasonable framework for viewing some of the ways people operationalize their aspirations. But, as seen throughout this study, some daughters, especially some in the aspirational low-earning category who are first-born or only children, are now playing very new roles in their natal families. This represents more than an appearance of status and more than a cultural shift alone. It is a structural reordering of gender relations within some particular segments of an enormous population group. As it occurs, actors within it are finding new openness for thinking differently about themselves and their roles, hopes, and opportunities. It will therefore be important in the future to do larger scale research on daughter-valuing families, and on valued daughters' life trajectories within the new would-be middle class, economically defined.

We now need to look at classes as income segments. A recent study identifies households earning between ₹18,000 and ₹36,000 per month as being middle-income (Kochhar 2015). This middle-income segment is only about 3 percent of India's population, dwarfed by what we can call the "would-be middle class". But while the low-income earning group, who are above poverty and earn between ₹3,600 and ₹18,000 a month per household, is the largest population segment, it is at only the higher level of this group—households earning ₹9,000 to ₹18,000 per month—that we find people who can manage above-subsistence purchases to project their socioeconomic aspirations (Kochhar 2015). Would-be middle-class families, then, are those who have enough income, though sometimes barely enough, to supply themselves with some of the accoutrements of a standard of living better than basic subsistence in order to be able to support their hopes of rising.

Social Reproduction

Feminist economists are concerned about the vast underbelly of the economy which is mainly managed by women, almost entirely unpaid and in the home. They point to ways in which global neoliberalism regressively reduces any assistance to women carrying out this essential, unpaid workload, and makes the income of women who are employed, whether formally or informally, less and less adequate (Gasper and van Staveren 2005, Williams 2006). While feminist economists often label this the "care economy," the economist Nancy Folbre's classic 1994 study uses the label "social reproduction," as I prefer to do. This is because there is a tendency in the language we use to cordon off sectors of the overall political economy where women are primarily located, rather than to place the combination of productive and reproductive roles played by women and men squarely in the center of the whole picture.

The family and household roles assigned to women make up basic parts of the process of social reproduction, writ large, and identified as the maintenance and reproduction of everyday life. These include childbearing, child rearing, family care, and household management, with all the physical, practical, and emotional costs and burdens upon a woman's body and well-being that these efforts entail. Well-known pieties and sanctions within custom and religion commend all these roles to women. But whether these are appealed to or not, the very idea of a woman as a housewife even if she is a career woman, too, is practically fixed. These roles are envisioned by my informants as all being so closely linked to biological reproduction as to require no involved explanation about why they are almost exclusively women's to shoulder.

What women's lives are for, and what their roles are supposed to be, have firmly included parenthood and child-rearing both in the past and in the present. To that end and for other vital family purposes, women's marriages are required, usually arranged by or in cooperation with their parents. Marriage is thus generally mandatory and inescapable. But at what age must marriage occur? The practice is responding very closely to the time of completion of education. To the extent that parents are supportive of a girl's gaining higher educational credentials, they are now willing to postpone her marriage to a later time than previously, so that the extension of the years of education a young woman undertakes goes hand in hand with an increase in her marriage age. To the extent that parents support her career ambitions, they are willing to postpone her marriage longer. (There is as yet only a small proportion of married female students.) The plan for a girl's marriage may place it immediately after she gains the credential she has been seeking, or hold it off for a couple of years further so that she can become established in her career. These are changes that urban parents are now making in their expectations and decisions about their educated daughters' futures.

The almost universal norm that a daughter must be married, rather than remaining single, assumes that the family should play a central role in arranging for this to happen, and with a couple of exceptions, this is true in the cases encountered here. There is social pressure on the family, sometimes gentle and sometimes intense, to make sure its daughters are settled in marriage; until this has been accomplished, the family cannot feel that it has fulfilled its duty to the daughter and to society. Chakravarti (2003), in her chapter provocatively titled "The Axis of Gender Stratification in India," relates all of this to the perpetuation of caste, as was referenced in Chapter 6.

Chakravarti's argument supports a picture of families and extended family groups as solidarity units, coalescing around a commitment to the continuation of caste privilege and exclusivity. This conception of families as solidarity units, groups of people both committed to one another's support and co-investors in each other's wealth, also owes much to Harriss-White (2003).

In our sample, however, we found a few inter-caste marriages of the parents. And there were several girls who disdained caste as a principle for choosing a mate. Yet the need to maintain a solidarity unit seemed powerfully to prevail among all the research subjects; but this need was not always supportive of caste as such in each particular case.

The young women I met expect themselves to be responsible for the household work of their marital homes, whether they carry out most of it or arrange to have it carried out by others. These still unmarried women students, though they are studying for lifelong careers, do not expect to have husbands who share equally in house-hold work. They hope to find one who will lend a hand. They plan to share the load with other women of the household. Most expect to have children, generally one or two, and to be primary caregivers or arrangers of care for them. They believe this care may be shared with other women in the household. These young women studying for careers are willing, even eager, to live in joint households with their prospective in-laws. They hope to find willing and supportive mothers-in-law, in particular.

These socially constructed, culturally sanctioned roles, still subscribed to by my research subjects, are not only matters of custom. As components of a system of social reproduction, seen in a materi-alist sense, they fall centrally within a mode of production which may shift its form and still contain these elements. The "housewife model" of gender can be transported and carried forward, even as the mode of production transforms. But this housewife model is a part of a system of social reproduction that may not so fully survive in the future, as the economic groundwork shifts further. This is not foreseen by any of the women I talked to. In the interviews and conversations with young women, their parents, and their professors, it was often said that the customs I have described are "inbred." There is a sort of biological trope inferred. To understand these customs differently requires a move away from the biological trope, toward an awareness of the social and historical constructedness of custom, and a clearer grasp of gender as a human construct. This awareness begins to be possible with exposure either to education influenced by Women and Gender Studies,[6] or to global models of comparison, or most likely to both.

Required marriage, insistence upon marriage taking place soon after education is completed, responsibility for household maintenance, and almost obligatory childbearing are all components of a system of social reproduction which is taken for granted, and which very few of the people with the prerequisites I selected can imagine will ever change. But it is possible, in fact likely, that changes taking place not only inside but also outside the household realm may come to alter that realm in more ways than people currently imagine.

Historical Transitions Revisited

The reproductive plan for today's young career-minded women, finding support from the parental generation on both the bride's and the groom's side for the raising of only one or two children, while the young adults pursue careers and seek advancement and self-expression, is a vision inextricably nested in the late stage of a demographic transition. Let us now review how this transition has proceeded and where it has reached thus far.

---

[6] See Mallarika Sinha Roy's (2014) essay on the far-reaching social and educational goals envisioned by the Women's Studies movement, aiming at the transformation of society.

Beginning in the 1970s, via improved health and material well-being, Indian society left behind the absolute and unavoidable predominance of death crises for families to have to deal with. A new phase began as mortality declined, when people could voluntarily reduce their completed fertility using modern methods. These unfortunately also came to include sex selective abortion, which has increased the masculinity of total births—but not by so much as to prevent the survival of many more girls than it destroys.

We are not in a good position to say what gender composition many parents might have originally wanted. Surviving daughters are partly valued in families according to their birth order and the gender composition emerging within the completed set of children. Many of the career-oriented young women I met, strikingly, are especially valued as the first child in the family. The largest part of their increased value, of course, is due to the education they are able to attain and then make use of. It is because of a remarkable change in the expected usefulness of educated daughters to their natal families, that more of them are being actively valued and invested in during this current era.

Once the 1970s began, the reign of death, which had weighed heavily on gender relations, receded, and an intermediate period in relation to women's position in society haltingly began. Between 1971 and 2001, in spite of women's increased life spans and rapidly growing levels of education, chances for most of them to build careers outside the home remained limited because economic opportunities were so very few. I would call these three decades a period of "Constrained Female Options." The cause for these options being so closely constrained, much more fundamentally than social conservatism and nationalism, was the very limited nature of economic opportunities during those years.

In the first decade of the 21st century, India entered the beginning of a different period in regard to opportunities for some young women just coming of age. Against a background of a century in which there had been very little change in the patriarchal/patrilocal structure and expectations even of urban families, this new period may be labeled as one of "Reknitting the Bonds of Loyalty." Using this rubric, we see some families moving from absolutely requiring sons, to grasping a new idea spreading among both the old and the new urban middle classes: the idea of encouraging and investing in educated, professional, and yet highly loyal daughters. In this most recent period, rich with new possibilities, some families are implicitly relying on women. This reliance rests with new emphasis on a family's own daughters (where previously it pointed exclusively in the direction of a family's daughters-in-law). A reknitting of loyalty bonds, a reformulation of solidarity units, capitalizing on the closeness between parents and their daughters, is occurring in some families for very particular, family-specific reasons. These are urban families; one or both parents have some education, but not as much as they would have liked. There are either no sons, or only one younger son. There are one or two daughters. These are families whose daughters are doing well in school, and for whom new, educationally qualified, professional opportunities appear realistic for those daughters to aspire to now.

In the mid-20th century, such families existed, but in minute numbers. The demographic regime of that time period contained high mortality, high corresponding fertility, and a homebound life for the great majority of those women whose families could afford to keep them, protect them, and fully utilize their services at home. Now there are more families with very few children, and some are of the newer, daughter-valuing type, even though these are not a dominant sector among urban middle-class families. Some of the constraints on female options have been reduced and new career opportunities have appeared due to globalization and economic growth. These options now appeal to families with daughters who are scholastically promising, particularly to those who have a daughter who is the eldest or the only child.

The bonds of loyalty in some families have thereby been rearranged; and it is clear that this is being been done partly for the purpose of maintaining a woman's extended natal family as a solidarity unit for a longer time. Ultimately, however, the family of a woman's in-laws will be the unit that she supports. Yet the ties with her parents promise to remain stronger than those traditionally sanctioned. Parents require children to help them in one way or another in their old age. Own daughters may be beginning to fill some of those roles. The solidarity of a daughter with her own parents may continue much more strongly than it used to after her marriage.

This rearrangement of family bonds that favors daughters is based on the demographic rates and resulting age structures of the moment. Future rates and age structures will continue to change. Some of the possible issues are discussed by McNey (2005). If gender roles do not change further as the demographic transition continues, young married women may face increasing rather than lessening responsibilities caring for family members. Older women may play useful roles in the household, including caring for children, as my research subjects hope they will; they will also survive to increasingly longer old ages, outstripping men due to lower mortality rates. So "having fewer children does not necessarily reduce women's caring role…. [Instead,] delayed childbearing may mean that the care required by old or frail dependents increasingly coincides with that demanded by children" (McNey 2005: 126–128; see also Croll 2006). These eventualities may certainly occur if gender roles and social supports do not change; but gender roles may be changing. In addition, professionalism among women as it continues to develop will change the willingness of older women to stay at home, as the young women of today become the elders. The in-laws will be out in the world pursuing their careers when their grandchildren come along.

Valued Daughters

In a starkly simplified dichotomy, there are two different world-views of daughter-valuing in India. Each of these two world-views is scattered all over India, relating to urbanization and class as well as to region and caste. One world-view values raising no more than one daughter, providing her with a dowry, sending her out in marriage to a family that needs a daughter-in-law, and reaping the sacred values and network connections that doing so brings. The other world-view values daughters (one or more) as potential objects of family pride in themselves, like sons. The level of education a girl attains, though impressive, does not make all the difference by itself; it is the family's intentions that are far more salient.

We must now briefly, but inevitably, discuss dowry. Going back through all the interviews, dowry was vociferously denied by everyone. It was even necessary for me to mention the tone of voice that young women and their parents used when this question arose. Dowry is understood to be one of the drivers of son preference, daughter discrimination, and sex-selective abortion, as well as being part of a socially dictated need to marry a bride into a higher status level (hypergamy) and then have her migrate to her husband's home, far distant from her parents. It seemed to me that my respondents were eloquently rejecting almost all of these social conventions.

Das Gupta (2009) finds that son preference may be beginning to unravel, and Guilmoto (2009) predicts an imminent improvement of sex ratios. Jeffery (2014) argues that the bulk of the evidence points in the opposite direction, but notices "some exceptions, such as a select stratum of educated cosmopolitan professionals" (2014: 177). That seems to me to be an important exception. Fernandes (2006), too, observes that educating girls for professions can pay off for urban parents, since highly educated, financially independent women can be married without any dowry.

A display of wealth can be important to people seeking to secure a higher social position to ratify their improved economic status (Saavala 2010, Brosius 2010). Dowry and lavish weddings are an important part of this display, a gamble that making good marriages for daughters will socially elevate their families. However, such a gamble can sometimes impoverish a family, due to continuing demands by in-laws for more dowry and cash flows after the wedding. But some urban families are making a different gamble. They are betting on a talented daughter's economic independence and continued support for them, and are letting her have a great deal more independent agency than formerly.

The current system of social reproduction limits women's independence to some extent, greater or lesser, after they marry. How will their extremely vocal professional aspirations tie in with this fact? They are honoring their embeddedness in their natal families now very highly, and they sincerely expect to do the same in their marital families later. But what will happen as they enter upon their careers and negotiate with all the players at home for conditions that will allow their professional success?

Pursuing their human rights in a neoliberal era, they may find more traction than their forbears did. It is almost inevitable that professional women, whatever background they spring from and however committed they are to the good of their families and communities, will also be oriented toward success as individuals. Women of older generations whom I know, who have succeeded in their professional ambitions, have all been able to build solid bourgeois lives with and for their families, however unselfishly abstemious a lifestyle they maintain. We may hope that these enthusiastic students adopt activist progressive positions and promote these with strong voices. But this will make them no less truly middle-class individuals. These are young women who demand to be heard, who want to make a difference and will actually be able to do so, in many ways that are yet to be observed.

How Much Difference Can Valued Daughters Make?

There may well be lifestyle and cultural spillovers to other groups, cities, and regions, from the example of lively young educated urban women believing in themselves. If their hopes are later curbed by poor job prospects and the prescriptive gender roles prevailing in marriage, their having developed such a strong sense of possibility may still tend to spread and influence others. For themselves, they will hold out for greater equality even in marital families where their wishes are strongly challenged. This generation of urban educated women, with hopes and plans for life-long professionalism, may put in place a pattern of expectations that pushes greater equality for women forward faster than it has moved in the past. This could well become possible if the economy resumes its rapid growth, spreading to new cities its demands for skills that continue to be accessible to educated women.

Can a young woman become a newly conscious self? (Can the subaltern speak?) Young middle-class women occupy a social location very different from those their mothers did at their ages—and they are very aware of this. A change has been made in the system of gender relations within their own families and family networks, and this does not escape them. Living as they do along the front margin of this visible change, they are conscious of it, even as they still emerge embedded in family, though not exactly in the same way as their mothers did. The embedded self is not always and forever an unconscious self. (Is there a pedagogy of the oppressed?) Running away from subordination, even as subject formation is occurring, young women see it and name it and lay claim to their own power to change it—only a little, perhaps; but this naming remains. Gender in itself becomes gender for itself; yet gender is nothing if not an embedded, socially constructed category. Seeing that it is so, a young woman may become conscientized; maybe more than her supporters ever intended.

There is a politics of personal negotiations within a family, and is it not necessarily a politics dependent upon upper-class cultural capital. Walking away from one kind of oppression, even while one's embeddedness in family is sustained, the emerging self becomes a mirror for the past, and for what the embedded category of gender used to be and no longer quite is. This awareness of the instability of categories is unsettling, even as it allows great excitement about one's own hoped-for future. And this exciting, unsettling awareness of the mutability of categories that had seemed immutable before is a depth charge, lurking under the surface, ready to be ignited in new and unexpected solidarities, new and unpredictable demands.

The visualization of women in India by scholars has in some cases remained stilted. Changes in women's agency occurring within their own emerging self-consciousness have not always been closely observed. "Their actions could be radical, but the representations of them were always as merely liberal or more typically as conservative ones" (Kumar 1994: 229). In contrast, there is a kind of knowledge "that locates the revolution within the subject, where the transformation of the world lies within the transformation of the self" (Kapur 2012: 350). This has been an important reason for writing this book, based upon the narratives of a number of unique and ardent young women in four cities.

In looking at an intersectional set of transitions leading to a new process of subject formation among young urban women in India, I must agree that "South Asian studies cannot proceed without taking cognizance of the subjectivity of women" (Kumar 1994: 3). In fact, twenty years after Nita Kumar wrote those words, this is so more than ever. Female autonomy and professional and personal agency are increasing for a larger subgroup of women than ever before, even if neither smoothly nor swiftly, even if not completely or in some absolute terms.

The legacy of female career ambition continues and is gathering force, with the possibilities now found in career-directed education, urban and global exposure, and the changing profile of possible employment in the increasing number of fields now considered professional. There may be few opportunities or inadequate personal growth actually available in some of these fields; jobs may be scarce, or not what they are meant to be; but these hoped-for possibilities will still generate a more consciously articulated self-identity. College women of promise are engaging in identity-building in their imaginations. As they prepare for life, their assertiveness capability in defining who they are has become strong and clear. The failures of Indian development and of the labor market, even if catastrophic, cannot completely deprive them of this fresh new sense of what their future lives can and rightfully ought to be.

9

Toward Gender Transformation

In this concluding chapter, I offer further thoughts on gender and the transformations it is now undergoing, though at a microscopic level within a vast and complex society; and I propose a pathway into the future that might bring about greater equity between the sexes. I continue pointing out issues raised in this book which could be taken up for further exploration by others. And I stress once again the deep historicity of this current time of gender change in relation to both past time and future time.

Professionalism and Marriage

Professional and semiprofessional occupations were the mark of a new class under the British. This class was notionally a new middle class, but these English-educated men actually formed a subservient comprador class, which socially functioned as an aspirational elite within Indian colonial society. The Sarkars (2007) have explained how members of this social segment somehow considered themselves as equivalent to the English middle class, even though, while performing services for the British, they were rooted in land revenue, rather than business. Drawn from the upper castes and the higher social strata, they were primarily Hindu. As a proportion of total population, this entire upper caste stratum was, and still is, a minority; as a proportion of that stratum itself, this new elite was, and still is, even more of a minority. Cutting the pie economically instead of socially, and referring to more recent times, Bardhan (1999) has rather pungently remarked, "the top decile or so in the income structure … for some reason is called the 'middle class' in India."

For the new English-speaking elite emerging within colonial society, family formation continued to be carried out within caste. Each caste was not only lodged within a larger Hindu social hierarchy but also had (and often still has) a hierarchy within itself prioritizing hypergamous marriages between the ranks, so that men of this new elite were a powerful magnet for families seeking marriage alliances via the offer of their daughters. To do so provided sacred values to the daughter-giving family (van der Veen 1972), as well as social connections within the higher ranks of the family's own caste, which were affirming their identities as part of the new elite.

Child marriage was almost universal for high-caste girls throughout the early process of new elite formation and consolidation. Startling age gaps between brides and grooms were more common than not (Forbes 1996). The men who constituted the new class were both educated and fluent in English, and considered as elite precisely for being so; the young girls being married off to them were not at all educated and did not know English. This pattern of extreme gaps in age, education, and linguistic ability continued until the reform movement began to take hold in the late 19th century. As that movement unfolded, daughters began to be allowed some education, though of a rather specialized, limited kind, for the purpose of providing elite men with compatible companions. Parents were now concerned to keep up with this new trend, as their children's marriages were being made to fulfill social status claims.

A small but remarkable change began to occur within the domestic space of these elite marriages themselves, giving more freedom of self-identity to young married men in relation to their elders (Walsh 2004). By having a more educated wife, a man gained status within his own extended family network. But Sinha (2012) notes that a changed masculine identity was also being forged here, one that concomitantly provided somewhat more agency to wives, as the young husbands themselves pulled away to some extent from older family norms and demands. Sinha makes the searching observation that this 19th century process began to de-center the gender binary (to however small an extent) from its strict formation in harmony with classical Sanskritic texts.

All of this was occurring in the new class that considered itself to be professional or at least semiprofessional. In providing services within the various branches of government under the British, many men were small office holders and clerks, holding bureaucratic jobs involving enormous amounts of duplicative paperwork. These jobs might have seemed to be low-level ones, had they not conveyed greater social and political power over the family networks of these men, and over people both equal and lower in the social hierarchy who needed government services, permissions, or aid. The stacks of paper and the requirement of numerous signatures for any request to get anything done remains a hallmark of governance today (Gupta 2012). Clerks might be fairly considered as working-class people in a class analysis solely based on functioning, as well as relation to means of production. But in a colonial context, where English education was required for clerks, such people became authorized gatekeepers at however a minor level. Service to the *huzur* had in any case had an honorable (even semi-elite) quality under governments in India, whether imperial, regional, or local, going back long before British rule began; and the habit of trying to marry daughters into the ranks of those who served in this way had a very long pedigree.

Paper pushing and clerking, even though they may be seen to have a certain dignity commensurate with other clean-caste occupations, ought properly to be considered working class. Then and now, such occupations prevail, and there are changes particularly in the caste and gender makeup of some such jobs under systems of reservations. But there are not enough changes in the work itself to consider some of it as properly professional at all. I have left out here any detailed consideration, however, of those occupations that were universally considered professional in the 19th century, and still are, such as law, medicine, and higher education, and have also omitted a close look at the business classes and their rise and central role during the same century. In the Hindu social system, these higher ranks of employment were all occupations that tended to be monopolized by the upper castes.

The spread of business as an occupation among the middle-caste (or the "upper") peasantry, along with these groups' movements to rise in status, however, became more forceful in the 20th century, leading later toward increased education and professionalization among their members as well. Suffice it to say that all these rising occupations and livelihoods attracted marriage alliance seekers, and tended with the reform movements of the late 19th and early 20th centuries to move toward more education for women. M. N. Srinivas (1966) tended to contrast the "Sanskritization" that was followed by aspirational groups (a process of attempting to improve the social status of a caste group by having it adopt more upper-caste practices than formerly) with "Westernization," seen as the alternative process of social change. I demonstrate here, however, that when gender is more carefully factored in, these two processes can be seen as historically (and they probably still are) rather closely combined.

We now need to look more closely at the question of marriage alliance itself, as an issue powerfully constitutive of, and constituted by, gender and hierarchical gender relations.

Gender, it needs to be repeated, is a social construct building upon sexual dimorphism. The fact that women have wombs, required for the biological reproduction of the species, has been referred to in many cultures in times past in relegating women to a subordinate social status. Even when not being confined to the home (if economically such confinement is a possibility), even when working outside, whether in employed roles or in the fields or in the most menial tasks imaginable, women are vastly disadvantaged compared to men. This disadvantage refers not only to their occupations, be they housewives or menial workers: women are subject to enormous violence and brutal domination, based on their biology and physical vulnerability. Women's sexual vulnerability has allowed almost all cultures, at some time in their history, to construct the female as temptress and moral weakling. Woman's vulnerability to rape, and the woeful and widespread prevalence of rape with almost complete immunity, has been used as a reason to shut her up at home, in order to protect and reserve sole access to her to the male selected to be her mate. And his access has been seen to be unlimited. The rule of men over women has been seen to be simply necessary for the preservation of culture and civilization, in a world where all outside men are potential threats.

A vulnerable, docile, and obedient daughter, not surprisingly, tends to be agreeable to her parents' arrangement of a marriage for her. Convinced (realistically) that dangers lurk for women, deeply attached to their parents by habits of affection and compliance, young women in most families cooperate without question in having arranged marriages within their families' caste and social preferences. In addition, as Patricia Jeffery sagely observes, "Economic independence is very elusive for women … their 'unemployment' is largely hidden within the home…. Young women, then, generally must comply with their parents' wishes for their marriage, not least because marriage remains their best chance of economic wellbeing" (Jeffery 2014: 179). But all of this is more particularly true for women who are being married very young; and India still has a large proportion of women who are married before age 16.

Age at marriage is a crucial topic. The importance of the period spent not being married cannot be overstated. Women will spend many decades married; but the decades and the extra years spent before being married are central to their self-identity formation, their hopes, and their character. Their relationships while still living with their parents as unmarried young adults can be increasingly assertive as well as respectful. The more years that elapse beyond puberty until marriage, particularly when a woman is becoming further educated for most of the elapsing years, the more favorable it is for her ability to express her own wishes in regard to her career, whom and when to marry, and about many important issues in the arrangement of her life and career after her marriage.

The Importance of Fathers

Who is a career-minded young woman's staunchest supporter? Before marriage, and sometimes even afterwards, it is often her father, with her mother following along in his wake. Why is this? Some men, even if from very traditional backgrounds, have given up the notion that a son is the sine qua non of the social reproduction of their family, writ small. The actual smallness of the family units they seek to sustain is an important consideration that we will look at.

I think of Neela's father, rejecting the very idea of a sex-selective abortion, and along with his attentive, intelligent wife, finding satisfaction in their small family of two daughters instead. This is a man from the Patidar community, once mainly comprised of farmers. In the 18th and 19th centuries, although some members of this Central Gujarat community held higher local offices as Desais and Amins under the various rulers of that region in those times, most community members were either large or small holders of land; many of them tilled the land themselves. In the late 19th century, subgroups of this community sought to become known as *ujalivasti,* clean-caste people, as a way of raising the status of their community into higher ranks in the caste system than being farmers or landholding peasants (Clark 1989a). That past effort has become blurred since the mid-20th century, when many Patidars moved into cities and took up urban business occupations, insisting that all along they have been members of the third Varna rank, Vaishya, rather than the fourth, or Sudra. This has been important to their sense of dignity: only the top three ranks in the ancient Varna system (Brahmins, Kshatriyas, and Vaishyas) were considered to be twice-born (dvijya) castes, also known as "clean castes," while Sudras were excluded from that honorific status and considered as merely workers. Now, of course, many caste groups in India that have remained identified as Sudras are benefitting by being classified as OBCs, and being allotted certain reservations set aside for that designation. Some ranks of the Patels are currently seeking OBC status, too, in ironic contrast to the fact that most of their subgroups are now fairly well off, some of them extremely so.

That current process of benefit-seeking does not apply to Neela's parents or to their forebears, who have carried a more dignified status for several generations. Neela's mother's father was a professor. Neela's father's father was a moderately large landholder in his village. Neela's father himself grew up mainly in Vadodara, after his parents relocated there from the village because of the greater educational opportunities for their children to be found in that city. He began an early career in banking and added education to it later, so as to rise to become a bank manager. This family is now far away from its village roots, visiting village relatives rarely and not feeling at home among them.

Neela's father would therefore not benefit from thinking of his two daughters mainly as social alliance material within his own caste. Clearly he did not think he required a son, either, to attract another family to send its daughter to his as a method of maintaining and even elevating the respect of his family. What this family's story seems to demonstrate is a change in gender relations going hand in hand with a considerable change in intra-caste relations. There is a loosening of the links within the caste that appears quite new. It compares sharply with the prevailing situation when Neela's mother was a young girl growing up in Hyderabad, when her father told her she must marry someone from their own community back home, and that this was more urgently required for her happiness than fulfilling her own wish to go to medical school and become a doctor. In other words, for a gender system change to occur in a family seems to require a change in the intra-caste priorities held by the head of a family. No doubt, for his priorities to have shifted so far, maintaining intra-caste relations must have lost some of its mandatory force within his branch of the community itself. Neela is set to become a fashion designer, and her elder sister, a dentist. These roles appear to be of greater interest to their parents than families they might form alliances with for social status purposes within their own caste.

Other families in my sample also had brotherless daughters who were being put forward as very important to be invested in and valued. In some others where sons were present, the daughter was the eldest and the son the youngest. "Why waste her talents, why consign her to marriage alone, when she can clearly shine in education and career, too?" It was also important in many of these families to groom the daughter for self-dependence, since resources for doing otherwise were scarce to nonexistent. "Why not do so with great pride?" These words (though not literal quotations) reflect the thoughts I gleaned from fathers themselves. Jaya's father was the first one I met. He and his wife were excited that Jaya (even as a second-year college student) was proving academically so talented that she could realistically imagine competing for a position in the Indian Administrative Service in a few years. This was an OBC family in Allahabad, in which the father's father had been a BDO and in which the father himself was a part-time administrative worker. While these roles indicate at least two or more generations of educated accomplishment coming out of a lower caste background, the economic condition of this family was now an anxious one. The parents and their four children lived in a tiny two-room house. The parents sat there with me and Jaya, speaking with great intensity. There was tremendous pride and resolve in their faces and voices. The way they treated and spoke about Jaya coincided with her glowing confidence.

I think also of the Vadodara father from Rajasthan, telling his accomplished 25-year-old, Priya, elder sister to two younger ones, "I am doing my best for you, *beta*!" He was working to find her a suitable partner who would allow her to elude the pressures of the relatives back home who were dead set against a career woman. This was a business family in which Priya herself was showing great business aptitude. The father and uncles who had moved to Vadodara all held Priya's skills and talents in high esteem. Caste mores would have to be modified in this marriage arrangement as well. Priya's mother was always receding into the background and covering her head, maintaining a tactful silence to maintain peace at times when Priya would speak out. The relatives in Rajasthan also said it was highly inappropriate for a woman's income to help maintain her family. These caste-based traditional practices could not prevail if Priya was to continue being who she had become. Whether this father or several others described in this book would be able to find a husband within the same caste for the daughter, while upholding her ambitions, was in question, but supporting her appeared to be their chief aim rather than maintaining their caste loyalties.

Why has caste loyalty apparently receded in some of these cases I observed? The way that times have changed for families is a topic that needs to be examined here. Generalizations abound regarding the supposedly increasing nuclearization of the family. This is a false perception. With extended life spans, there are more relatives living together now than that word implies that there should be. Whether it is a young woman's grandparents, uncles and aunts who live in her parental household, or the expected set of relatives she will live with once married, these configurations are usually considered joint families. This is a partial misnomer and can give rise to a misperception as well. What seems to be happening is a drawing in of the boundaries to a smaller and closer set of relatives who depend on one another; the flattening out of the octopus-like shape of the wider solidarity network, which has had its own strict internal hierarchy as well as its many tentacles. The wider network I am talking about is one of authority and rules as well as people. Some of its authority is being sapped out of it.

The importance of fathers to the women's movement needs to be noted now. I want to suggest ways that women can act to support those men who are willing and able to support women. However, the mere suggestion that men who support their daughters' career ambitions should be thought of as in any way feminist may seem objectionable: this idea may seem simply to reinforce an ideology of patriarchy. It is as though this whole narrative composed of young women's stories tends toward support of a patriarchal ideology. For if a daughter requires the guidance of her father and the cooperation of her husband, how far is this different from the Laws of Manu? In addition, it is perfectly clear that the encouragement offered by many of the fathers I describe has been motivated by more than pure goodwill toward the daughter. It serves the family interest to encourage the daughter, and she knows this and honors it. Much has been written in these pages about the deeply embedded female agency this implies. If a woman's agency is at the behest of family interest, is it truly agency at all?

I return here to the fluent articulateness of the young would-be journalist in Allahabad, Raina, who spoke of young men of her acquaintance changing their tone toward women, uneasily, but out of support for their sisters, seeing that their mothers had a constricting burden that these young men would not like either their sisters, or their wives-to-be, to bear. Raina speaks of using her skill of persuasion with her brother, her "guy friends," and her mother; for her father, she only expresses profound appreciation for his unstinting latitude. I also refer back to Rani, a Marwari girl with an elder brother whose family lives in Mumbai. She is a young woman who may not quite get to have a career, but who is effervescently expressive about freedom. Like many of my subjects, she declares, "I am so grateful to my parents! It is they who have given me all this freedom!" It is contingent freedom, yes; but not brutally contingent. The contingent freedom of educated young women is still a breath of fresh air. As they look about them at women's lives more generally, they breathe deep of it.

A self-modifying patriarchy, one might argue, is still an obstacle to the aims of the women's movement; and this position would be partially true. Patriarchy has shown itself to be slippery and adaptable across modes of production that have been transformed again and again across phases of history. Attempting to label the mode currently in force in India is a complicated task, since there are several. I will make this attempt at least: India's urban landscape is partially dominated by a postcolonial/neocolonial, neoliberal, globally dependent, unevenly developing mode. I leave off any attempt to label small-town and rural landscapes, deferring to the admirable concision of Harriss-White (2003). But in the urban landscape where this current research has taken place, there are families registering the productive mode's transformation in their family structures and behavior and values.

Saying anything favorable about a neoliberally modified urban patriarchy arouses concern, too, among all of us who rightly seek a progressive and thorough going sociopolitical transformation. But let us consider the infamous Delhi rape case of 2012. While at least one post has labeled the victim Jyoti/Nirbhaya as being the perfect neoliberal subject, it is the parents of the dead woman who even more indelibly come into view by virtue of their thoughtful, tragic interviews on film (*India's Daughter*). Consider the massive, insistent, continuing protests of that year, and their many spinoffs in the years and months since. It is clear that as well as youth activism, we now have a vast swath of middle-class and would-be middle class urban families insisting upon rights, safety and access for their daughters; items none of which would have or could have been insisted on so publicly, by so many, just one generation ago.

How can women support men who are able to support women, and in so doing use the modified patriarchy as a stepping stone toward greater gender equality? If we refer approvingly to fathers who support and sponsor their daughters, it is then very important to help expand their legacy among young men. One of the ways I have seen this done at two of the universities I visited in this research is through enlisting male students in Women and Gender Studies courses and encouraging eye-opening discussions between the sexes in the classes. Another has been the enrolling of young male activists in movements calling for change on the many fronts where gender justice is urgently needed.

Future Population Trends

Starting with this view of a self-modifying urban patriarchy, then, we ought to build upon it with more than just the image of protest and outrage that has not gone away since the Delhi rape case. Startlingly, we ought also to build upon it with a reminder that this is a time of rapid, unprecedented fertility decline. It is a time of rapid scaling down of the size and extendedness of family solidarity units (though not of the phenomenon of relatives living jointly); and it is also a time of a kind of economic development which is not providing enough employment. What it does have is a professional sector that is growing and diversifying. Though that sector is small when projected upon the enormous canvas of the nation, its outsized productivity is vital. And the professional and semi-professional opportunities that may be opening up for women now (even if these become somehow curtailed later) are even more vital to a larger view of the long future that stretches out ahead.

What lies ahead is the eventual flattening of India's population growth curve. The leveling off of population growth to a rate hovering close to replacement may not occur for another hundred years or more (or, it may actually occur in just a few decades). Because it is rather far in the future, its onset is hardly discussed or even imagined. But when a population no longer significantly grows, many social and political changes will take place. After levelling off at the level of replacement (about two children per woman, on average, including all childbearing-aged women in the population whether they ever have children or not), and then remaining at a similar size level for a considerable period, population size may then actually begin to decline. The coming slowdown of population growth will both accompany and also lead to continuing changes in the status of women, coupled with, to many, a surprisingly rapid decline of now unquestioned pro-natal social factors and cultural practices.

Almost the entire current social fabric is now pro-natalist, oriented toward an unquestioned mandate for all people to have children of their own to provide the multiple values Indian families hold dear. After getting married, for example, almost any young professional woman soon begins to hear the drumbeat: When are you going to have a baby? Young married professional women whom I know, relishing their careers with the enthusiastic support of their husbands, are hearing this call. It may come from one side of the marriage more than the other, or from both together, or even from several sources, including siblings, neighbors, and distant relatives. Such couples may then be catapulted into using their dual professional incomes to buy their own apartments, so as to distance themselves somewhat and carry on with their chosen occupations and practices. This is a quite different outcome than what seems to be serenely expected by almost all of my unmarried, student inter-view subjects. They envision living with in-laws as a great source of support to them. In general, this is the expected context of their currently expressed desire to have children as they continue their careers. But after graduating, beginning their careers, and marry-ing career-supporting spouses, will they feel the same? I remember Revathi, a married woman in Bengaluru, who said—while she was pregnant—"Not only kids are important. Career is too." She and her husband were just then setting up household without members of the older generation, even while honoring both sets of parents and continuing to live near enough to them to have frequent interactions.

Pro-natalist expectations regarding women's roles and duties are practically an ironclad necessity in a high-mortality society. Very high mortality demands high fertility in recompense. We saw this clearly in Chapter 3. But when mortality remains quite high in some levels of society, while becoming quite low in others, this creates a different effect. With its extremes of wealth and poverty, and with aspirational classes growing faster (due to the economic advancement of some) than the growth of population as a whole, India will continue to experience the reduction of many time-honored pro-natalist factors, starting at first among its upper and middle classes. These factors, especially the most essentializing notions about women and their fixed roles in household maintenance, childcare, and elder care, will then increasingly begin to fade among India's struggling would-be middle-class groups, who are now rapidly curtailing their fertility. For a period of time, poorer economic strata and regions may continue to reproduce in above-replacement numbers, following pro-natalist gender practices and still valuing sons over daughters. This may not last forever, however; and only broad social policies supporting families and children will be able to modify a serious decline in net reproduction that could ultimately take place under the actual anti-natalist conditions that may arise.

Pro-natalism, the valuing of women as mothers while devaluing them as individual persons; the prioritizing of sons, and the disproportionate sex ratios: all of these go together to support not only patriarchy but also misogyny. But these two categories are not the same as one another. The first, patriarchy, is a set of interlocking institutions. The second, misogyny, is a malignant attitudinal and behavioral tendency. The first holds sway as a part of the basic structure of society, maintaining as a key value an authoritarian and gender-differentiated vision of how families ought to be structured. The second holds nothing so dear as belittling and despising what it despises. The first can sometimes hold love within it; the second is based on hate. When do the two mingle, putting both patriarchy and misogyny together in play, and causing mayhem?

Population and economy have much to say about this. When economic growth stalls, overall or in large sectors of the economy, and when its benefits are more and more unevenly distributed among the population, political bitterness develops and finds outlets in prejudice, discrimination, hatred, and violence. When neoliberal global export-oriented sectors take pride of place in the nation's productivity index and a resulting privileged class carelessly grows richer and more thoughtless, these tendencies are exacerbated. When local and global corporate actors buy influence over governments and suppress, undermine, and dismantle state social provisioning, these malign trends continue to grow. The only real escape valve is an appropriate and thoroughgoing realignment of the entire system of social reproduction.

Society Reproducing Itself

Here I want to correlate two different uses of the term social reproduction, the predominantly cultural use of it, paired with one mainly based on a materialist analysis. The cultural idea of social reproduction is brightly illuminated in the work of Bourdieu, who gets due recognition also as, at bottom, a materialist (Jain 2006). For the social reproduction he highlights is actually the reproduction of class society along with the reproduction of privilege, through cultural means. Featured in his viewpoint, however, there is a kind of monopoly of these cultural means, making it nearly impossible for those not belonging to privileged social categories to access them. But I have contested this view as applied to current patterns of urban Indian social change, and argued that new cultural capital is now being created all the time out of a rich combination of inputs. It is important that women's education is one of these, but it is only one.

Young urban educated women have been observed in this book collecting, manipulating, and recreating in different forms these varied source materials of new cultural capital: the influences of their urban locations; their exposure to the world via media and the internet; the novel hopes of their families; the mentorship of their professors; the impact of women's studies; the existence of interesting new professions; the use of policies undertaken by government over previous decades; movements for gender justice; and new measures for redress of injustices done. Thus the cultural capital being newly created both by and for women today is of quite a different kind than what existed even just two decades ago. It includes a culture of change, and a culture of politics, awareness, and activism.

A more materialist analysis of social reproduction delineates it as part of the structure of a given mode of production, diagramming it as describing the social relations of reproduction appropriate to that particular overall productive regime (Clark 1987). I have acknowledged here, however, that one can really only make a stab at describing today's modes of production at all, and that there is certainly more than one prevailing in current day India. Earlier I had summoned a vision of a globally interpenetrative mode of production, using Meillasoux's 1981 work as a reference for postulating the ways that the more developed parts of the world system penetrate the less developed ones and prey off of them, maintaining an extreme demographic imbalance. In the intervening decades, this framework has not yet become completely inaccurate, though its pattern is sharply changing. And in this age of global hyper-communications and globalized neoliberalism, that pattern has become more complicated, more ramified.

What is most germane to the study being reported on in this book is that Indian family life today seems to be reproducing some of its customs and usages in new forms. To take a very straightforward topic, let us look at how children are being raised today in regard to educational attainment and future options by gender. Many surveys show how much more education children now are getting than their parents' generation completed. The National Family Health Survey for 2014–2015 is currently underway, with no results yet available at this writing; its data would be particularly pertinent to this study. But the one completed in 2006 revealed that of the nation's 20 to 24 year olds in that year, 43 percent of males and 31 percent of females had completed at least ten years of schooling, while the figures for 40–44 year olds (roughly approximating the next generation up, that of the younger people's parents) showed that only 30 percent of males and 14 percent of females had finished 10th standard. India's educational trajectory over time is thus shown as very impressive; children on average are becoming much better educated than their parents, with girls rushing to close the gender gap with boys. The same survey also tells us that in the *urban* populations of all ages,

38 percent of men had completed at least 10 years of school while 29 percent of women had done so. That nine point gap between urban men and women is even smaller than that of either of the two age pairs (pertaining to urban and rural populations lumped together) that were just mentioned above.

Children now are getting more education than their parents ever completed, and a large share of them are still continuing their schooling so that their own completed educational attainment will eventually outstrip that of their parents' generation even more widely. Increases for girls outstrip those for boys. This educational gap between the generations may be seen as somewhat analogous to the sharp salary differential between a mature father and young adult daughter that I showed in one of the Bengaluru cases. What will such changes mean in terms of the productive and reproductive relations within family units, groups, and regions? What will they mean as an influence on family culture?

Child Rearing and Gender Construction

Let us consider the process of gender construction under current conditions of rapid fertility decline and shrinking education gaps between the sexes, as education for all advances. Sinha (2012) suggested that in the 19th century, the mere beginning of educational change already amounted to a tiny step taken in the direction of deconstructing the gender binary in its strict form. What does it mean, following the same logic, that the shrinkage of the education gap has continued and speeded up? If it means that more daughters are becoming seen in more families and locations as equal persons with sons, with equal family rights and responsibilities, then according to the same logic the gender binary itself is increasingly weakened by the eradication of gender gaps in education. The very difference between sons and daughters lessens.

There becomes, then, less sanction for gender to continue to hold sway as a socially constructed category based on women's mandatory role in biological reproduction. The mandate for all women to bear children may weaken; the mandate for all daughters to be settled in marriage may fade. The requirement for a wife to be a housewife may become very questionable. This being a time of continuing fertility decline, a child of either sex can provide the solidarity and care a family needs. Parents may eagerly approach the fertility level that produces zero population growth as they welcome one or two children as enough (and the old slogan pops inevitably into one's head). A notion that this process of population growth reduction down to replacement level (or even lower) will seriously stall over the long term, due to the influence of traditional Indian family norms, or even due to the current sway of neoliberalist ideologies, may very well be misplaced.

Increasingly egalitarian child rearing in a realigned and stripped-down system of social reproduction within households, with families struggling to provide for both economic provisioning and human care via more equally shared roles, might create an urgent new politics for a new society. The very goals of society and politics could be changed by the joint advance of greater gender equity and very low population growth. With a new politics voicing its demands, a fairer production and distribution system might be evolved in tune with the newly urgent need for maintaining social reproduction in an era when population size had stabilized.

This is only a vision, containing only a few parts of the puzzle of fundamental change, leaving out all the hard issues of economics and governance and political struggle, but it is perhaps at least a suggestive one. As Nivedita Menon (2009: 371) has declared, "feminist politics ... requires dense contextual analysis to remain both relevant and critical." Dense contextual analysis needs to examine many different intersectional parts of the total context: historical, economic, demographic, social, and cultural. Leaving out some of these contexts may foreshorten the scope of one's understanding of what will be needed in the future. It is to be hoped, then, that this study has provided, in miniature, the kind of dense contextual analysis that will be required by a feminist vision of the future.

Bibliography

Agarwal, Bina, Jane Humphries, and Ingrid Robeyns, eds. 2005. *Capabilities, Freedom, and Equality: Amartya Sen's Work from a Gender Perspective*. New Delhi: Oxford University Press.

Agnew, Vijay. 1979. *Elite Women in Indian Politics*. New Delhi: Vikas Publishing.

Amin, Sajeda. 2006. "Implications of Trade Liberalization." In *Trading Women's Health and Rights? Trade Liberalization and Reproductive Health in Developing Economies*, edited by Caren Grown, Elissa Braunstein, and Anju Malhotra. London and New York: Zed Books.

Banerjee, Nirmala. 2011. "A Note on Women as Workers." In *Mapping the Field: Gender Relations in Contemporary India*, edited by Nirmala Banerjee, Samita Sen, and Nandita Dhawan. Kolkata: Stree.

Bannerji, Himani. 2001. *Inventing Subjects: Studies in Hegemony, Patriarchy and Colonialism*. New Delhi: Tulika Books.

Bardhan, Kalpana. 1990. *Of Women, Outcastes, Peasants, and Rebels: A Selection of Bengali Short Stories*. Berkeley: University of California Press.

Bardhan, Pranab. 1999. *The Political Economy of Reform in India*. New Delhi: NCAER.

Basu, Alaka Malwade. 1996. "Girls' Schooling, Autonomy and Fertility Changes: What Do They Mean in South Asia?" In *Girls' Schooling, Women's Autonomy and Fertility Change in South Asia*, edited by Roger Jeffery, and Alaka Basu. New Delhi: SAGE Publications.

Baviskar, Amita, and Raka Ray, eds. 2011. *Elite and Everyman: The Cultural Politics of the Indian Middle Classes*. New Delhi: Routledge.

Bourdieu, Pierre. 1977. *Outline of a Theory of Practice*. Cambridge: Cambridge University Press.

Bourdieu, Pierre. 2010. *Distinction*. London: Routledge.

Bourdieu, Pierre, and J. C. Passeron. 2000. *Reproduction in Education, Society and Culture*. London: SAGE Publications.

Brosius, Christiane. 2010. *India's Middle Class: New Forms of Urban Leisure, Consumption and Prosperity*. New Delhi: Routledge.

Chakravarti, Uma. 2003. *Gendering Caste: Through a Feminist Lens.* Calcutta: Stree.

Chanana, Karuna. 1996. "Educational Attainment, Status Production and Women's Autonomy: A Study of Two Generations of Punjabi Women in New Delhi." In *Girls' Schooling, Women's Autonomy and Fertility Change in South Asia,* edited by Roger Jeffery and Alaka M. Basu. New Delhi: SAGE Publications.

Chatterjee, Partha. 1989. "The Nationalist Resolution of the Women's Question." In *Recasting Women: Essays in Colonial History,* edited by Kumkum Sangari, and Sudesh Vaid. New Delhi: Kali for Women.

Chaudhuri, Amit. 2009. *The Immortals: A Novel.* New York: Alfred A. Knopf.

Clark, Alice W. 1987. "Social Demography of Excess Female Mortality in India: New Directions." *Economic and Political Weekly* 22 (17). (*Review of Women Studies*).

————. 1989a. "Limitations on Female Life Chances in Rural Central Gujarat." In *Women in Colonial India: Essays of Survival, Work and the State,* edited by J. Krishnamurty. New Delhi: Oxford University Press.

————. 1989b. "Mortality, Fertility, and the Status of Women in India, 1881–1931." In *India's Historical Demography: Studies in Famine, Disease and Society,* edited by Tim Dyson. London: Curzon Press.

————. 1993. "Analysing the Reproduction of Human Beings and Social Formations." In *Gender and Political Economy: Explorations of South Asian Systems,* edited by Alice W. Clark. New Delhi: Oxford University Press.

Clark, Alice W., and T. V. Sekher. 2007. "Can Career-Minded Young Women Reverse Gender Discrimination? A View from Bangalore's High-Tech Sector." *Gender, Technology and Development* 11 (3): 285–319.

Croll, Elisabeth. 2006. "The Intergenerational Contract in the Changing Asian Family." *Oxford Development Studies* 34 (4): 473–491.

Damaske, Sarah. 2011. *For the Family? How Class and Gender Shape Women's Work.* New York: Oxford University Press.

Das Gupta, Monica. 2009. *Family Systems, Political Systems, and Asia's "Missing Girls": The Construction of Son Preference and its Unravelling.* Policy Research Working Paper 5148. World Bank.

Das Gupta, Monica, and P. N. Mari Bhat. 1997. "Fertility Decline and Increased Manifestation of Sex Bias in India." *Population Studies* 51 (3).

Das Gupta, Monica, and Li Shuzhou. 1999. "Gender Bias in China, South Korea and India 1920–1990: Effects of War, Famine and Fertility Decline." *Development and Change* 30 (3): 619–652.

Datta, Kusum. 2011. "Women's Studies in India." In *Mapping the Field: Gender Relations in Contemporary India,* edited by Nirmala Banerjee, Samita Sen, and Nandita Dhawan. Kolkata: Stree.

Dube, Leela. 2001. "Kinship and Gender in South and Southeast Asia: Patterns and Contrasts." In *Anthropological Explorations in Gender: Intersecting Fields*, edited by Leela Dube. New Delhi: SAGE Publications.

Dyson, Tim. 2010. "Growing Regional Variation: Demographic Change and Its Implications." In *Diversity and Change in Modern India: Economic, Social and Political Approaches, Proceedings of the British Academy, No. 159*, edited by Anthony F. Heath and Roger Jeffery. Oxford: Oxford University Press.

Dyson, Tim, Robert Cassen, and Leela Visaria, eds. 2004. *Twenty-First Century India: Population, Economy, Human Development, and the Environment.* Oxford: Oxford University Press.

Edmeades, Jeffrey, Anju Malhotra, and Margaret Green. 2008. "Gender Inequality and the Demographic Dividend." Paper delivered at the 2008 meetings of the Population Association of America, New Orleans.

Elson, Diane. 2006. "Women's Rights and Engendering Development." In *Feminist Economics and the World Bank: History, Theory and Policy*, edited by Edith Kuiper and Drucilla K. Barker. Oxford: Routledge.

Everett, Jana, and Mira Savara. 1993. "Organizations and Informal Sector Women Workers in Bombay." In *Gender and Political Economy: Explorations of South Asian Systems*, edited by Alice W. Clark. New Delhi: Oxford University Press.

Fernandes, Leela. 2006. *India's New Middle Class: Democratic Politics in an Era of Economic Reform.* Minneapolis: University of Minnesota Press.

Folbre, Nancy. 1994. *Who Pays for the Kids? Gender and the Structures of Constraint.* London: Routledge.

Forbes, Geraldine. 1996. *Women in Modern India.* The New Cambridge History of India, IV.2. Cambridge: Cambridge University Press.

Ganesh, Kamala. 2001. "Maps for a Different Journey: Themes in the Work of Leela Dube." Introductory essay to Leela Dube, *Anthropological Explorations in Gender: Intersecting Fields.* New Delhi: SAGE Publications.

———. 2005. "Fields of Culture: Conversations and Contestations." In *Culture and the Making of Identity in Contemporary India*, edited by Kamala Ganesh and Usha Thakkar. New Delhi: SAGE Publications.

Ganguly-Scrase, Ruchira, and Timothy J. Scrase. 2008. *Globalisation and the Middle Classes in India: The Social and Cultural Impact of Neoliberal Reforms.* Oxford: Routledge.

Gasper, Des, and Irene van Staveren. 2005. "Development as Freedom— and as What Else?" In *Amartya Sen's Work and Ideas: A Gender Perspective*, edited by Bina Agarwal, Jane Humphries, and Ingrid Robeyns. Oxford: Routledge.

Government of India. 2011. *Census of India*. New Delhi.

Government of India, Ministry of Education and Social Welfare. 1974. *Towards Equality*. Report of the Committee on the Status of Women in India. New Delhi.

Government of India, Ministry of Health and Family Welfare. 2006. *National Family Health Survey-3*. New Delhi.

Government of India, Ministry of Human Resource Development. 2011. *All-India Survey on Higher Education 2010–11*. New Delhi.

———. 2013. *Educational Statistics at a Glance*. New Delhi.

Government of India, Ministry of Labour and Employment. 2011. *Statistical Profile on Women Labour 2009–11*. New Delhi.

Government of India, Ministry of Statistics and Programme Implementation. 2011. *Selected Socio-Economic Statistics, India 2011*. New Delhi.

Grant, Monica J., and Jere R. Behrman. 2010. "Gender Gaps in Educational Attainment in Less Developed Countries." *Population and Development Review* 16: 1.

Guilmoto, Christophe Z. 2009. "The Sex Ratio Transition in Asia." *Population and Development Review* 35 (3): 519–549.

Gupta, Akhil. 2012. *Red Tape: Bureaucracy, Structural Violence, and Poverty in India*. Durham: Duke University Press.

Harriss-White, Barbara. 2003. *India Working: Essays on Society and Economy*. Cambridge: Cambridge University Press.

Hart, Caroline Sarojini. 2012. *Aspirations, Education and Social Justice: Applying Sen and Bourdieu*. Bloomsbury Academic.

Heitzman, James. 2005. *Network City: Planning the Information Society in Bangalore*. New Delhi: Oxford University Press.

Hobsbawm, Eric. 1962/1996. *The Age of Revolution, 1789–1848*. New York: Vintage Books.

———. 1975/1996. *The Age of Capital, 1848–1875*. New York: Vintage Books.

———. 1989. *The Age of Empire, 1875–1914*. New York: Vintage Books.

International Institute for Population Sciences. 2008. *District Level Household Survey-3*. Deonar, Mumbai.

Jain, Sheena. 2006. "Bourdieu's Theory of Symbolic Traditions and Innovations." In *Reading Bourdieu in a Dual Context: Essays from India and France,* edited by Roland Lardinois and Meenaksh Thapan. New Delhi: Routledge.

Jeffery, Patricia. 2014. "Supply-and-demand Demographics: Dowry, Daughter Aversion and Marriage Markets in Contemporary North India." *Contemporary South Asia* 22 (2): 171–188.

Jejeebhoy, Shireen. 1991. "Female Literacy in India: The Situation in 1991." *The Journal of Family Welfare* 37 (3), September.

Kabeer, Naila. 1999. "Resources, Agency, Achievements: Reflections on the Measurement of Women's Empowerment." *Development and Change* 30 (3).

Kapur, Ratna. 2012. "Hecklers to Power? The Waning of Liberal Rights and Challenges to Feminism in India." In *South Asian Feminisms*, edited by Ania Loomba and Ritty A. Lukose. Durham: Duke University Press.

Katzenstein, Mary Fainsod. 1978. "Toward Equality? Cause and Consequence of the Political Prominence of Women in India." *Asian Survey* 18 (5).

Kaur, Ravinder. 2008. "Dispensable Daughters and Bachelor Sons: Sex Discrimination in North India." *Economic and Political Weekly* 43 (30).

Kochhar, Rakesh. 2015. *A Global Middle Class Is More Promise than Reality.* Washington, D.C.: Pew Research Center.

Koggel, Christine M. 2005. "Globalization and Women's Paid Work: Expanding Freedom?" In *Amartya Sen's Work and Ideas: A Gender Perspective,* edited by Bina Agarwal, Jane Humphries, and Ingrid Robeyns. Oxford: Routledge.

Krishnaraj, Maitreyi, Ratna M. Sudarshan, and Abusaleh Shariff, eds. 1998. *Gender, Population and Development.* New Delhi: Oxford University Press.

Kuiper, Edith, and Drucilla K. Barker, eds. 2006. *Feminist Economics and the World Bank: History, Theory and Policy.* Oxford: Routledge.

Kumar, Nita. 1994. "Introduction." In *Women as Subjects: South Asian Histories,* edited by Nita Kumar. Charlottesville: University of Virginia Press.

———. 2007. *The Politics of Gender, Community, and Modernity: Essays on Education in India.* New Delhi: Oxford University Press.

Kumar, Radha. 1993. *The History of Doing: An Illustrated Account of Movements for Women's Rights and Feminism in India, 1800–1990.* New Delhi: Kali for Women.

Lardinois, Roland, and Meenakshi Thapan, eds. 2006. *Reading Bourdieu in a Dual Context: Essays from India and France.* New Delhi: Routledge.

Liddle, Joanna, and Rama Joshi. 1986. *Daughters of Independence: Gender, Caste and Class in India.* New Brunswick: Rutgers University Press.

Lloyd, Cynthia B., ed. 2005. *Growing Up Global: The Changing Transition to Adulthood in Developing Countries.* Washington, D.C.: National Academies Press.

Majumdar, Manabi. 2011. "From Access to Attainment: Girls' Schooling in Contemporary India." In *Mapping the Field: Gender Relations in Contemporary India,* edited by Nirmala Banerjee, Samita Sen, and Nandita Dhawan. Kolkata: Stree.

Mari Bhat, P. N. 1989. "Mortality and Fertility in India, 1881–1961: A Reassessment." In *India's Historical Demography: Studies in Famine, Disease and Society*, edited by Tim Dyson. London: Curzon Press.

McNey, Kirsty. 2005. "The Implications of the Demographic Transition for Women, Girls and Gender Equality: A Review of Developing Country Evidence." *Progress in Development Studies* 5 (2): 115–134.

Mehta, Hansa. 1981. *Indian Women*. New Delhi and Baroda: Butala & Company.

Meillasoux, Claude. 1981. *Maidens, Meal and Money: Capitalism and the Domestic Economy*. Cambridge: Cambridge University Press.

Menon, Nivedita. 2009. "Sexuality, Caste, Governmentality." *Feminist Review* 91.

Miller, Barbara D. 1981. *The Endangered Sex: Neglect of Female Children in Rural North India*. Ithaca: Cornell University Press.

Mukhopadhyay, Swapna, and Ratna M. Sudarshan, eds. 2003. *Tracking Gender Equity Under Economic Reforms: Continuity and Change in South Asia*. Ottawa: International Development Research Centre; and New Delhi: Kali for Women.

Nath, Kamala. 1965. "Urban Women Workers: A Preliminary Study." *The Economic Weekly* September 11, 1405–1411.

National Institute of Public Cooperation and Child Development. 2010. *Statistics on Women in India 2010*. New Delhi.

Nielson, Kenneth Bo, and Anne Waldrop, eds. 2104. *Women, Gender, and Everyday Social Transformation in India*. London: Anthem Press.

Nussbaum, Martha. 2001. *Women and Human Development: The Capabilities Approach*. Cambridge: Cambridge University Press.

———. 2011. *Creating Capabilities*. Harvard: Harvard University Press.

Nussbaum, Martha, and A. K. Sen, eds. 1993. *The Quality of Life*. Oxford: Clarendon Press.

Oza, Rupal. 2006. *The Making of Neoliberal India*. New York: Routledge.

Palriwala, Rajni. 1994. *Changing Kinship, Family and Gender Relations in South Asia: Processes, Trends, Issues*. Leiden: University of Leiden.

———. 1996. "Negotiating Patriliny: Intra-Household Consumption and Authority in Northwest India." In *Shifting Circles of Support: Contextualizing Kinship and Gender in South Asia and Sub-Saharan Africa*, edited by Rajni Palriwala, and Carla Risseeuw. Walnut Creek: Altamira, a division of SAGE Publications.

Patel, Tulsi. 2006. *Fertility Behaviour: Population and Society in a Rajasthan Village*, 2nd ed. New Delhi: Oxford University Press.

Patel, Tulsi, ed. 2007. *Sex-Selective Abortion in India: Gender, Society and New Reproductive Technologies*. New Delhi: SAGE Publications.

Poonacha, Veena, and Meena Gopal. 2004. *Women and Science: An Examination of Women's Access to and Retention in Scientific Careers*. Mumbai: Research Centre for Women's Studies, SNDT Women's University.

Premi, Mahendra K. 2006. *Population of India in the New Millennium: Census 2001*. New Delhi: National Book Trust.

Radhakrishnan, Smitha. 2011. *Appropriately Indian: Gender and Culture in a New Transnational Class*. Durham: Duke University Press.

Ray, Raka. 1999. *Fields of Protest: Women's Movements in India*. Minneapolis: University of Minnesota Press.

Ray, Raka, and Seemin Qayum. 2009. *Cultures of Servitude: Modernity, Domesticity, and Class in India*. Stanford: Stanford University Press.

Roy, Srila. 2014. "New Subalterns? Feminist Activism in an Era of Neoliberal Development." In *Women, Gender, and Everyday Social Transformation in India*, edited by Kenneth Bo Nielson and Anne Waldrop. London: Anthem Press.

Rustagi, Preet. 2013. "Changing Patterns of Labour Force Participation and Employment of Women in India." *The Indian Journal of Labour Economics* 56 (2): 215–241.

Saavala, Minna. 2010. *Middle-Class Moralities: Everyday Struggles over Belonging and Prestige in India*. Hyderabad: Orient Blackswan.

Sahni, Rohini, and V. Kalyan Shankar. 2011. "Girls' higher education in India on the road to inclusiveness: on track but heading where?" *High Education* 63: 237–256. (Springer Science and Business Media, published online).

Sarkar, Tanika, and Sumit Sarkar, eds. 2007. *Women and Social Reform in Modern India, A Reader*, Volume II. Ranikhet: Permanent Black.

Searle, Llerena Guiu. 2013. "Constructing Prestige and Elaborating the 'Professional': Elite Residential Complexes in the National Capital Region, India." *Contributions to Indian Sociology* 47 (2).

Sekher, T. V., and Neelambar Hatti, eds. 2010. *Unwanted Daughters: Gender Discrimination in Modern India*. Jaipur: Rawat Publications.

Sen, Amartya. 1999. *Development as Freedom*. Oxford: Oxford University Press.

———. 2009. *The Idea of Justice*. New Delhi: Penguin Books.

Shah, A. M. 2002. *Exploring India's Rural Past: A Gujarat Village in the Early Nineteenth Century*. New Delhi: Oxford University Press.

Singh, Supriya, and Mala Bhandari. 2012. "Money Management and Control in the Indian Joint Family across Generations." *The Sociological Review* 60 (1), February.

Sinha, Mrinalini. 2007. "Gender in the Critique of Colonialism and Nationalism: Locating the 'Indian Woman'." In *Women and Social Reform in Modern India: A Reader*, Volume II, edited by Tanika Sarkar and Sumit Sarkar. Ranikhet: Permanent Black.

———. 2012. "A Global Perspective on Gender: What's South Asia Got to Do with It?" In *South Asian Feminisms*, edited by Ania Loomba and Ritty A. Lukose, 356–371. Durham: Duke University Press.

Sinha Roy, Mallarika. 2014. "Disciplining Gender and Gendering Discipline: Women's Studies in Contemporary India." In *Women, Gender, and Everyday Social Transformation in India*, edited by Kenneth Bo Nielson and Anne Waldrop. London: Anthem Press.

Srinivas, M. N. 1966. *Social Change in Modern India*. Berkeley: University of California Press.

Taylor, Charles. 1989. *Sources of the Self: The Making of Modern Identity*. Cambridge: Harvard University Press.

Taylor, Phil, Premilla D'Cruz, Ernesto Noronha, and Dora Scholarios. 2014. "From Boom to Where? The Impact of Crisis on Work and Employment in Indian BPO." *New Technology, Work and Employment* 29 (2): 105–123.

Thapan, Meenakshi. 2006. "Habitus, Performance and Women's Experience: Understanding Embodiment and Identity in Everyday Life." In *Reading Bourdieu in a Dual Context: Essays from India and France*, edited by Ronald Lardinois and Meenakshi Thapan. New Delhi: Routledge.

———. 2007. "Adolescence, Embodiment and Gender Identity: Elite Women in a Changing Society." In *Urban Women in Contemporary India: A Reader*, edited by Rehana Ghadially. New Delhi: SAGE Publications.

Van der Veen, Klaas W. 1972. *I Give Thee My Daughter: A Study of Marriage and Hierarchy among the Anavil Brahmins of South Gujarat*. Assen, Netherlands: Van Gorcum & Company.

United Nations, Office of High Commissioner for Human Rights. 1948. *Universal Declaration of Human Rights*. Geneva.

Visaria, Leela. 2006. "Fertility Change." In *Twenty-first Century India: Population, Economy, Human Development, and the Environment*, edited by Tim Dyson, Robert Cassen, and Leela Visaria. Oxford: Oxford University Press.

Waldrop, Anne. 2012. "Grandmother, Mother and Daughter: Changing Agency of Indian Middle-Class Women, 1908–2008." *Modern Asian Studies* 46 (3): 601–638.

Walsh, Judith E. 2004. *Domesticity in Colonial India: What Women Learned When Men Gave Them Advice*. Lanham: Rowman & Littlefield.

Webster's New World Dictionary. 1960. Cleveland: The World Publishing Company.

Williams, Mariama. 2006. "Why Feminist Economists Should Pay More Attention to the Coherence between the World Bank and the WTO." In *Feminist Economics and the World Bank: History, Theory and Policy*, edited by Edith Kuiper and Drucilla K. Barkar. Oxford: Routledge.

Index

feminine role, 140
feminism, 10
feminist, 26, 82
feminist analytical orientation, 9
feminist approach, 11
feminist economists, 159
feminist historiography, 9
feminist politics, 186
feminist protest and activism, 28
feminist social history, 9
fertility levels, 44
financial crisis, 103

gender change, 28
gender construction, 185
Gender Studies, 29
gender transformation, 170
genealogy, women's ambition, 144
generational shift, 3
Ghosh, Aurobindo, 20
girl students in higher education, 107
globalized employment, 141
globalized labor market shifts, 142
globalized neoliberalism, 120

harmonious family support system, 106
historical transitions, 162
historical vital rates, India, 38
human rights, 167

Independence Movement, 17, 20, 25
India, historical vital rates, 38
Indian economy, 102, 107
Indian Women (Mehta), 60
insurance, 23
internet, 145, 147
interviews

Abhita, 150, 155
Amrita, 147–149
Anjana, 40–41
Neela, 121–126, 127, 132, 152, 175–176
Priya, 79, 151–151, 155
Raina, 152, 153
Rani, 79, 150
Revathi, 104–105
Sarita, 151
Tanika, 152
Urmila, 152–153
Vasanti, 152

Jeffery, Patricia, 174

Karve, D.K., 58

life expectancy, 37, 42

Maharaja Sayajirao University of Baroda, 59
male-dominated nationalism, 16
male–female relations, 94
marriage, 64–65, 66, 67, 70–73, 75, 78, 83, 84, 86, 88, 91–93, 95, 106, 110, 111, 113–117, 144, 146, 148–151, 155, 160–162, 165, 167, 170, 171, 173, 174, 176, 177, 181, 186
in-laws, 71
maternal mortality, 39, 43
Menon, Nivedita, 186
middle-class aspirations, 158
middle-class identity, 157–159
middle-class women, 145–146, 168
Ministry of Human Resource Development, 47

About the Author

Alice W. Clark is a historian and scholar of gender and society in India, who has taught history and women's studies at several universities in the San Francisco Bay Area, including Santa Clara University. She most recently was the instructor on "The Culture of India" for the University of California-Berkeley Extension Online. After completing her Ph.D. in Comparative World History from the University of Wisconsin, she pursued Indian women's issues under postdoctoral fellowships in demography. She has consulted on diversity and women's issues in several countries, given numerous invited lectures, and lived in India for lengthy periods. With valued professional daughters and grandchildren of her own, she is also involved, along with her husband, in social reproduction from a personal perspective. In her spare time she enjoys being by the ocean, nature walks, conversation, folk music, reading, and visiting art museums and galleries.